Digital Images in Education:
Realising the Vision

Edited by Leona Carpenter and Caren Milloy
with Lorraine Estelle and Jane Williams

Published by JISC Collections

© JISC Collections

Published by
JISC Collections
Brettenham House
5 Lancaster Place
London
WC2E 7EN

JISC Collections is funded by the Joint Information Systems Committee
(JISC)

Date of Publication: October 2007
Publishing History: 1st Edition

British Library Cataloguing in Publication Data
A catalogue record for this book is available from the British Library.

ISBN: 978-0-9557185-0-2 Digital Images in Education: Realising the Vision

Printed by Woods Group Ltd, Chippenham, United Kingdom

Foreword

I was very pleased to be asked to write a foreword to this book. As someone who has been involved in the work of the Joint Information Systems Committee (JISC) almost since its inception, I have seen the way in which the Committee has been a powerful force for the innovative development of Information and Communications Technology (ICT) applications in learning, teaching, research and reach-out within the UK's higher and further education sectors. Nowhere has this been more evident than in content creation and delivery. The present publication continues the JISC tradition of visionary pathfinding towards new futures and solutions in the field. As always, the main issue is not technology: it is rather the social, cultural, legal and organisational challenges that need to be met. This book sets out to address them.

'A picture's meaning can express ten thousand words': so the 'Chinese proverb' states. The rise of the internet and digital media has opened up significant possibilities for the delivery of message and meaning through visual rather than text-based media. The potential is enormous, but the challenge of realisation significant. The opportunities and the issues surrounding digital images are two themes that permeate this book. The potential impact of digital delivery of images is another; the needs of the user – and the need to find out what they are and how to satisfy them – the fourth, and most important, aspect of current and future work. The provision of access to collections and the ability to ensure their widespread and appropriate availability through easy-to-use yet sophisticated discovery tools is of paramount importance, underpinned by effective responses to image collection content and access

ugees Arrive
Getty Images, via Education Image Gallery.

requirements, the coordinated development and management of collections and the resolution of particular issues – notably the legal and the ethical – surrounding some collections of material.

The publication is timely. The JISC's aim is to build collections and communities to that 'tipping point' where images will be central to the information environment, not least because of the availability of critical masses of easily accessible quality material. Much progress has already been made in the area, not least thanks to the work done by and through JISC, as evinced by the descriptions of the Digital Picture, CLIC, Digital Images Archiving and other projects and studies. But, as a result, many questions have arisen – whether technical, cultural, economic, legal, social or even ethical (as in the case of patients' records) – and it is now necessary to look at common approaches and solutions to ensure that the vision of meaningful, pervasive, efficient and cost-effective digital delivery of images can be realised; and here we are talking about truly global ways forward in a landscape that goes beyond individual subject areas, sectors and even countries.

At the moment, however, it is potential rather than reality, not least because of the high level of variety and complexity in digital image creation, preservation, collection management (including selection processes) and access. Reading through the contributions to this book, it is clear on the one hand that the challenges are significant – for example the issues surrounding ownership and Intellectual Property Right alone – but, on the other, that the work being undertaken or overseen by the JISC's Images Working Group and others is identifying present good practice and achievement and setting out the necessary next steps. In this context, the fact that many of the authors are summarising user-survey work is important.

The book indicates how digital communities and sectors can work towards the goals described here, overcoming the barriers to access and usage and ensuring that common solutions become embedded within learning, teaching and research communities, and beyond. The book, then, does not just set out the vision or provide a synthesis, but disseminates information and knowledge in the area and, most important of all at the present time, aims to influence policy, practice and funding decisions. It is thus essential reading, and I commend the book wholeheartedly to the attention of everyone within the JISC community and beyond with an interest in or a responsibility for images, hoping that they will give the Images Working Group and the JISC their full support as we begin to realise the vision.

Professor David Baker
Chair, JISC Content Services Committee
Summer 2007

Acknowledgements

First, I owe special thanks to my co-editors Caren Milloy (for all the work and for picking up the ball whenever I dropped it), Lorraine Estelle (for a steady hand on the tiller and timely contributions), and Jane Williams (for clear-sightedness and robust, timely input).

My co-editors and I wish to thank and to acknowledge the contributions of the members of the Images Working Group (IWG), including some past members, for initiating and developing the vision for digital images in UK post-16 education and research. Participants in the report authors' synthesis workshop helped to shape this book, as well as the first steps to take forward the realisation of the vision. Each of you is identified in the contributors list, but special thanks is due to Seamus Ross, IWG Chair, for proposing this book.

In addition, Caroline Taggart's proofreading was attentive and informed by her knowledge of the subject area. Stuart Parkin did sterling work as our picture researcher, a particularly sensitive and essential role in a book about digital images. And finally, we would like to acknowledge the participation and support of the many individuals and institutions in the UK higher and further education community and the broader cultural heritage sector who supported or participated in the studies reported here and in the IWG development of the vision.

Leona Carpenter
July 2007

Contents

List of Figures

List of Images

Contributors

Sheila Anderson
(chapter 6 author, Digital Images Archiving
Study co-author, synthesis workshop
participant)
Director
Arts and Humanities Data Service (AHDS)
Executive
Kings College London

Tony Austin
(Digital Images Archiving Study co-author)
formerly Technical Manager, Archaeology
Data Service,
University of York

David Baker
(preface; Chair, JISC Content Services
Committee)
Principal
The College of St Mark & St John (MARJON)

Rachel Bruce
(chapter 7 co-author)
Programme Director, Information
Environment
JISC Executive: Development
Kings College London

Helen Cameron
(chapter 5 co-author, CHERRI Project
co-leader)
Director
Medical Teaching Organisation
University of Edinburgh

Leona Carpenter
(editor, chapter 2 author, chapter 7
co-author, Images Working Group past
member)
Freelance

Angelo Conti
(Images Working Group member)
Head of ILT Development
Swansea College

Hugh Dailly
(Images Working Group past member)
Curriculum Development Officer, JISC RSC
Scotland, North & East
Edinburgh Telford College

Stuart Dempster
(chapters 2 and 7 contributing author)
Project Director Strategic Content Alliance
JISC Executive: Development, Kings College
London

Catherine Draycott
(chapter 2 contributing author, Images
Working Group past member)
Head of Photographic Library
Wellcome Library

Mick Eadie
(Digital Images Archiving Study co-author)
Collections and Systems Manager
Deputy Director, AHDS Visual Arts
University College for the Creative Arts

Rachel Ellaway
(chapter 5 co-author, CHERRI Project
co-leader, synthesis workshop participant)
e-Learning Manager
College of Medicine and Veterinary Medicine
University of Edinburgh

Lorraine Estelle
(co-editor, chapter 7 co-author, synthesis
workshop participant, Images Working
Group member)
Chief Executive Officer
JISC Collections

John Falconer
(Images Working Group past member)
Jerwood Curator of Photography
The British Library

Catherine Grout
(chapter 7 co-author, synthesis workshop
participant, Images Working Group
member)
Programme Director, e-Content
JISC Executive: Development
Kings College London

Helen Hockx-yu
(chapter 7 contributing author, chapter
6 introduction, past JISC Programme
Manager)
PLANETS Project Manager
The British Library

Neil Jacobs
(chapter 7 contributing author, chapters 4 and 5 introduction, synthesis workshop participant)
Programme Manager, Information Environment
JISC Executive: Development
University of Bristol

Graeme Laurie
(chapter 5 contributing author, CHERRI Project consultant)
Co-director of the Arts and Humanities Research Council (AHRC)
Professor of Medical Jurisprudence
Research Centre for Studies in Intellectual Property and Technology Law
University of Edinburgh

Rick Loup
(Images Working Group co-opted member)
Multimedia Services Development Officer
EDINA
Edinburgh University Data Library

Margaret Maxwell
(chapter 5 contributing author, CHERRI Project consultant)
Senior Research Fellow in Primary Care Mental Health
General Practice section, Division of Community Health Sciences
University of Edinburgh

Jonathan Miller
(chapter 4 co-author, CLIC Project Manager, synthesis workshop participant)
Technical Officer
Learning Technologies Group
University of Oxford

Caren Milloy
(editor and chapter 3 introduction, Images Working Group member)
Collections Manager
JISC Collections

Balviar Notay
(chapter 7 contributing author, Images Working Group member)
Programme Manager, Information Environment
JISC Executive: Development
Kings College London

Malcolm Polfreman
(Digital Images Archiving Study co-author)
Information Officer
Arts and Humanities Data Service (AHDS) Executive
Kings College London

Rebekah Pratt
(chapter 5 contributing author, CHERRI Project consultant)
Research Fellow
General Practice section, Division of Community Health Sciences
University of Edinburgh

Andrew Prescott
(Images Working Group member)
Director of Humanities Research Institute
University of Sheffield

Mike Pringle
(Images Working Group past member, chapter 3 author, chapter 1 co-author, Digital Images Archiving Study co-author, synthesis workshop participant)
Director, AHDS Visual Arts
University College for the Creative Arts

Julian Richards
(Images Working Group Member)
Director, Archaeology Data Service,
Department of Archaeology
University of York

Peter Robinson
(chapter 4 co-author, CLIC Research Officer)
Manager, Multimedia Specialist
Learning Technologies Group, University of Oxford

Michael Ross
(chapter 5 co-author, CHERRI Project co-leader)
Clinical Lecturer in General Practice and Fellow
Medical Teaching Organisation, University of Edinburgh

Seamus Ross
(Images Working Group Chair, synthesis workshop participant)
Director of HATII
University of Glasgow

Rupert Shepherd
(chapter 4 co-author, CLIC Research Officer
– Museums)
Manager of Museum Documentation
Ashmolean Museum
University of Oxford

Amber Thomas
(chapter 7 contributing author)
Programme Manager, Information
Environment
JISC Executive: Development
University of Bristol

Philip Vaughan
(chapter 7 contributing author)
Programme Manager, Information
Environment
JISC Executive: Development
University of Bristol

Jane Williams
(co-editor, chapter 1 co-author, Images
Working Group member)
Director eLearning
Centre for Medical Education
University of Bristol

Mark Williams
(Images Working Group past co-opted
member)
Access Management Outreach Co-ordinator
JISC Executive: Services and Outreach
Kings College London

Andrew Wilson
(Digital Images Archiving Study co-author)
Preservation and Projects Manager at AHDS
2005-2006

Grant Young
(chapter 4 co-author, consultant to CLIC
project)
Technical Research Officer
Technical Advisory Service for Images (TASI)
Institute for Learning and Research
Technology (ILRT),
University of Bristol

Karla Youngs
(Images Working Group co-opted member,
chapters 1 and 4 co-author, consultant to
CLIC project)
Director
Technical Advisory Service for Images
(TASI),
Institute for Learning and Research
Technology (ILRT)
University of Bristol

A Vision for Images in Education

To provide the UK education community with long-term access to the digital image resources that it needs, in a variety of convenient, flexible and easy-to-use ways. Ideally, provision should: be free at the point of use; comply with common open standards; cover the broadest range of possible subject areas; have copyright clarity; be sustainable; and support maximum usage at all levels of teaching, learning and research.

Full Earth
NASA.

Robot Arm Over Earth with Sunburst
NASA.

Such a vision will provide UK Higher and Further Education communities with:

- an open-access virtual reservoir of images
- the basis for a permanent asset for education
- clarity of rights and usage
- a framework that would facilitate the sharing and finding of digital images
- access to images covering a wide range of subjects
- facilities for all levels of tertiary education
- an additional facility/service provided and integrated with the JISC Information Environment
- a resource for future generations

The vision is based on a need to deliver a smart, innovative, evolutionary and financially appropriate approach to the provision of digital images to the JISC education community. Recognition that we need this sort of strategic approach is itself not new, and a review of activities, papers and reports developed over the last five years has contributed to this proposal. The following list outlines the basic assumptions that prompted the JISC's Images Working Group (IWG) to think about and plan new directions:

- digital technology has reached a useful and usable level of maturity
- demand for the right kind of image content within the HE and FE communities is high
- competition to provide resources is becoming increasingly fragmented
- duplication of effort is expensive, wasteful and confusing
- risks to the community of not acting strategically are becoming more apparent
- opportunities to do something exciting and original in this area are available
- the community is eager to engage and embrace something new
- and, most importantly, if we are to move forward effectively we must have a strategy that is appropriate to, and endorsed by, the community

Achieving the vision

The JISC Images Working Group (IWG) has identified several objectives that can help towards the achievement of the vision:

- To develop plans for facilitating/leading a change of culture in the provision, access and use of digital images in education. Plans are required that help the community move away from provider-led, controlled management of resources and towards an open, sharing culture wherein development of resources is led by direct user involvement and genuine needs.

- To initiate a feasibility study into the idea of a support service that would enable a national network of digital images to evolve into a virtual reservoir. Such a service, perhaps aligned to current JISC activity in Digital Repositories and Preservation and Resource Discovery, would facilitate and manage the 'joining-up' of any number of image sources – repositories, portals, services, upload tools, harvesting mechanisms and access points – and would enable the UK education community to deposit, share, discover and access the images it needs. The service would also ensure long-term access to images whether they have been purchased (or licensed) for, or deposited by, the community. Furthermore, the management of the virtual reservoir would facilitate the forging of alliances with other national organisations and, possibly, with commercial providers of image collections.

- To develop processes and facilities that enable organisations and individuals to interact more fully with the images of the virtual reservoir. The reservoir should be capable of exploiting novel internet approaches (e.g. those commonly termed Web 2.0[1]) to ensure that growth and development are essentially led, and governed, by the education community itself for its own, vastly differing and changeable, needs.

- To focus, initially, on a candidate community where needs are to some extent understood and definable, and where many image sources are already available; this approach would permit a more fluid development of the virtual reservoir while catalysing digital image activity in accordance with the vision. The IWG believes that the art and cultural heritage sector is an appropriate and receptive community for such an approach. Lecturers and researchers in this area have a tradition of using image material effectively in teaching, learning and research, and the most immediate way to make successful inroads towards the vision might be through meeting some of the specific image requirements of

---

1   O'Reilly, Tim, What Is Web 2.0: Design Patterns and Business Models for the Next Generation of Software, see: **www.oreillynet.com/pub/a/oreilly/tim/news/2005/09/30/what-is-web-20.html**

this community. This could be done by funding institutions/individuals to digitise their own resources (as with previous and current JISC digitisation programmes) on the condition that they provide copies of these images to the virtual reservoir, and also by forging alliances to seed collections from other organisations; for example, national galleries or, if appropriate, commercial image libraries.

- To identify the mechanisms necessary to support the continued development and maintenance of the virtual digital-image reservoir and to strive to fill gaps in the resource coverage where clear needs and possible solutions can be identified.

- To consider how such approaches will, at some point in the future, be an important part of a seamless facility that allows the contribution of, or access to, digital images of all types and in all subject areas across the UK and in liaison with other wider, European or international, initiatives.

This vision is aligned to the first three JISC strategic aims: to deliver innovative and sustainable ICT infrastructure, services and practice that support institutions in meeting their mission; to promote the development, uptake and effective use of ICT to support learning and teaching; and to promote the development, uptake and effective use of ICT to support research. It can be achieved by building on the considerable experience of JISC Services such as the Arts and Humanities Data Service (AHDS), the Technical Advisory Service for Images (TASI) and the Jorum learning object repository service; and in conjunction with JISC Information Environment development programmes such as the digital repositories and preservation and digitisation programmes.

Community needs

'The problem as I see it is that lecturers certainly want and need to make more use of images in their teaching, but have their hands tied by the copyright restrictions and fee demands imposed by the majority of services. Free collections maybe OK for downloading a picture for a one-off lecture, but most lecturers are, legitimately, quite wary about downloading images for use in the VLE or printed course materials. The other aspect of the problem is that the sort of images English lecturers might use is very varied. They might need anything to illustrate the historical, geographical or cultural background to a text, as well as material to do with texts and authors themselves. We cannot therefore point to a single collection of images which might form the basis of a collection.'
Jane Gawthrope, Manager, HE Academy English Subject Centre

Jane Gawthrope's comment summarises the frustrations that the community feels in respect of the use of digital images, and elucidates the reasoning underlying the IWG's vision, which is founded on a growing belief throughout the JISC community that provision of online resources must be led by the 'actual' needs of a defined user community. This means much more than simply assuming which images should be provided, particularly when such assumptions are based on the perceptions of bodies external to the community, whether they be offering delivery services, software development or access to resources. Accordingly, the vision recommends that all digital-image collection, and associated tools and facilities, are based on and influenced by members of the education community themselves.

About the JISC Images Working Group

The IWG is one of six Collections Working Groups that advise and guide JISC Collections[1] in the acquisition and licensing of high-quality online content. JISC Collections (the trading name of the JISC Content Procurement Company Limited) is a service supported by JISC to negotiate with publishers of online resources and with owners of digital content, on behalf of further and higher education. The Collections Working Groups act as informers to JISC Collections regarding the needs of the education community and as think-tanks when evaluating new resources.

The IWG brings together representatives from the UK higher and further education communities, as well as co-opted members from JISC-funded services such as TASI[2] (the Technical Advisory Service for Images), EDINA[3] and the AHDS[4] (Arts and Humanities Data Service). Each member of the IWG has expertise in the area of digital images and the use of such images within teaching, learning and/or research. The IWG and JISC Collections work closely with the JISC Executive, and with the Development group[5] in particular, on the context within which these resources are made available to the further and higher education community. JISC Collections reports to the JISC Content Services[6] committee four times each year. In 2005 the committee endorsed the work of the IWG in developing this vision.

References

1. JISC Collections
    http://www.jisc-collections.ac.uk/
    JISC Collections. From Wikipedia, the free encyclopedia
    http://en.wikipedia.org/wiki/JISC_Collections

2. Technical Advisory Service for Images (TASI)
    http://www.tasi.ac.uk/

3. EDINA – providing national online resources for education and research
    http://edina.ac.uk/

4. AHDS (Arts and Humanities Data Service)
    http://ahds.ac.uk/

5. JISC Development group
    http://www.jisc.ac.uk/aboutus/about_jisc/structure/development_group.aspx

6. JISC Content Services committee
    http://www.jisc.ac.uk/aboutus/committees/sub_committees/jcs.aspx

Chapter 1

Digital Image Provision: The Vision in Context

Mike Pringle, Jane Williams and Karla Youngs, with members of the Images Working Group

ra Australis

The original JISC Images Working Group (IWG)[1] vision document, *Steps Towards a National Vision for Images*, was released with the intention of provoking discussion and eliciting thoughts and suggestions from various JISC Collections[2] Working Groups[3] and also from a number of other relevant individuals and organisations. Therefore, in addition to the core vision as developed at that time, the document provided background on past IWG and JISC[4] image-related activity, proposals for new studies and recommendations for further developments. This chapter is based on that original document, with consideration of the responses it received, and details the context and a framework for achieving the vision of the IWG for future digital-image provision within the JISC community.

Consultation with the community

One of the four foundations of modern living

© The Museum of English Rural Life.

The vision for digital images in education was inspired, driven and informed by a belief that provision should be based on the real needs of the various elements of the digital-image-using community. Consequently, the IWG, along with JISC Executive, determined that consultation with relevant communities was imperative in order to develop the vision. At the core of the consultation, a series of studies was commissioned, each of which was designed to elicit responses from specified communities who use digital images within their practice. Each of the studies is represented by a chapter in this book, but they are summarised here:

the Digital Picture[5]: a future for digital images in UK arts education. A national overview of issues, and potential solutions, relating to the use and impact of digital image collections within higher education and research institutes, and associated organisations, with a focus on visual arts.

Bridging the Gap: investigating Community Led Image Collections (CLIC)[6]. A study to research and define a suitable organisational and technical model to support the deposit and sharing of community image collections within further and higher education.

Towards a Clinical Commons: using clinical recordings in academic non-clinical settings. A study (under the name of CHERRI[7] – Common Healthcare Educational Recordings Reusability Infrastructure) to define a possible framework for the deposit of sensitive and clinical (medical, dental and health-related) recordings.

Digital images archiving[8]. A study to explore the issues, both cultural and technical, that affect the long-term preservation and sustainability of digital images for educational use.

In addition, a ***Visual and Sound Materials Portal***[9] ***demonstrator project*** was commissioned to undertake the development of an image portal demonstrator, based on the recommendations of the JISC PIXUS[10] project. A further feasibility study was undertaken as the first phase of this project, which was to adopt all JISC IE[11] standards and work to point users towards time-based media and still images – including those licensed for the JISC community, those available 'free' on the internet and those generated within the academic and publicly-funded community.

As well as the studies named above, and in relation to the idea of focusing initially on a candidate community, the IWG consulted with the Heads of Art History departments in UK higher education institutions to discover what their needs are in terms of digital art collections. Three issues emerged from this consultation:

- The range of images required by art historians in educational institutions cannot be satisfied by the acquisition of any one main image collection, due to the diversity of courses offered and the wide variety of specialist research.

- The majority of institutions have their own slide collections that have been developed over decades to meet the specific needs of their academics and students. Currently only a few institutions might be in a position to fund the digitisation (and acquisition/clearing of necessary rights) of these collections and so preserve them for the future and make them more accessible to a wider community.

- Departmental and art library budgets are under considerable pressure and many respondents feel unable to commit to ongoing subscription fees for commercial collections.

These three apparently straightforward statements offer a very brief look at some of the perceived problems faced by a specific community, but they are, in fact, indicative of many deeper and more complicated issues that face not only the art history sector but anyone who wishes to use digital images for educational purposes. In simplistic terms, the key points underlying these issues are:

Diversity of needs. The sheer extent of diversity of perspectives, and therefore potential solutions, of users of digital images is vast: huge differences fill every level of even the most specific subject matter; the different needs of the volume of subject areas in what we call teaching, learning and/or research communities is incalculable. Meeting such needs will never be achieved through a single point of access or by a solo venture of any description.

Limitation of resources. Those members of teaching, learning and research communities who have traditionally used images in their practice have built up huge stocks of images that met their individual needs. However, making the switch to a world where digital image supply is sufficient for educational needs requires a huge investment in time, effort and funds. Issues such as image quality, colour management, digitisation processes, copyright or metadata and the training needed can be extremely complex and, often, pose insurmountable problems

Sustainability. With budgets stretched, continual development of teaching, learning and research needs, and an ever-changing technical environment, decisions for image users (and budget holders) are complicated by the fact that many online image facilities, like many other online facilities, can appear to be transient. Also, change is often governed by the collection or website owner rather than the user; and, because an owner's priorities may differ from the user's, there can sometimes appear to be a lack of educational dependability, security and consistency.

These three themes recurred frequently in the results of the studies outlined above. However, the studies also confirmed that the solution to such issues, and many other related issues, lies, fundamentally, in taking a different approach to the way we do things. In particular, it is clear that many of the problems relating to access to digital images are dominated by human factors: they are *cultural*, not technological.

the Digital Picture project, which focused on the digital-image needs of the visual arts, revealed that 72% of respondents to a survey felt that they should have the training, time and tools to create digital images themselves; while 47% suggested that their institution should deal with the issue, perhaps via an intranet, institutional repository, Virtual Learning Environment or through the library. A compromise view was that of a one-stop shop (subject-based) augmented by local facilities. However, the IWG believes that such an approach will not work in isolation: the construction of a website/portal/

Turkey Display
© Getty Images, via Education Image Gallery.

gateway will not resolve the complex human issues that lie behind the paucity of appropriate digital image access. *the* Digital Picture proposes that a more fluid, evolutionary approach might be required. Community members may be better served through a series of diverse components and methods which, through working together with common aims, could gradually move towards a future where digital image needs will be met. After all, many of the images that are required are already available in digital form (or soon will be) and a huge proportion of them are, theoretically at least, already in the public domain or 'free' for educational use.

Process not product

Solutions for providing easy access to images may be about *process* not *product*; the priority, not to build a one-stop website, but to figure out how, as a community, we can share our image information efficiently. One major cause of the current situation is the fact that very few people are working together towards a solution: most providers are governed by their own, individual drivers rather than the broader needs of the community. They are trying to meet known user needs, but only for their own target users, or in line with constraints of funding, politics, branding or available images.

This is indicative of an underlying, much broader issue in education culture – essentially, many of the people or organisations who should be part of the solution are in competition with one another and with everyone else. For a solution to emerge, the culture itself needs to change. This vision has emerged because the JISC exists to help the community, to act as facilitator for the amelioration of exactly such issues.

The notion of competition was also apparent in the results of the CLIC project. CLIC identified that the biggest barrier to sharing images among individuals, institutions and communities is lack of trust. Technical barriers can be overcome, but a technical solution in no way guarantees the success of image sharing. The CLIC project, like *the* Digital Picture, concluded that the problem is social, not technical. Collection providers need to be able to trust that the material they provide will be used only in ways that they find acceptable, and that their ownership and IPR will be respected.

By-the-community, for-the-community solutions for resource provision in tertiary education have been, and continue to be, developed with the support of JISC programmes. Experience within the e-Learning[12] and Digital Repositories[13] programmes has particular relevance to community-based digital-image activities. JISC has invested in the tools to support community creation of learning materials, and Jorum[14] provides an example of what can be achieved in support of the sharing of community-created resources. While Jorum is not specifically an image repository, its content does include images. Many of the cultural issues related to resource sharing that had to be addressed in developing the Jorum service echo those raised in digital-image studies.

A unified approach to community-led image access

The CLIC project suggests some practical ways in which people can work together towards a common aim: support for local development of core, copyright-cleared, subject-based collections; national initiatives driven by subject-based demand; community-owned repositories; a register of visual teaching material needs; the adoption of Creative Commons[15] licences, or a limited number of Creative Commons-style licences; facilities for securing sensitive images; a series of community-owned directories of image collections, with minimal system administration; partnerships for sharing subject material; and, perhaps, a national collection of material the main role of which would be to supply images that are not available elsewhere, under suitable licence terms.

Further complexity was identified by the CHERRI study, looking at the use of clinically sensitive recordings for academic non-clinical settings (CRANCS), particularly in respect to the conflict between creating a completely safe environment for the use of CRANCS without sacrificing their utility or aspects of a 'greater good'. Prohibiting the use of CRANCS for teaching and research would undermine the effectiveness of both and could have a detrimental impact on the competence of future healthcare professionals.

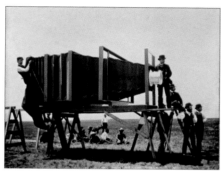

George R. Lawrence's (1869-1938) Mammoth Camera, c.1900 (sepia photo) by American Photographer, (20th century)
©Private Collection/ Photo © Boltin Picture Library/ The Bridgeman Art Library.

As with the two previously mentioned studies, CHERRI also identified the need for a common approach, outlining the need for a common activity framework to support the acquisition, storage and use of CRANCS. Indeed, CHERRI suggests that such a framework is absolutely essential for any large-scale and dynamic exchange of these kinds of recordings. Without greater normalisation of procedures, the continued use of CRANCS will create further risks and problems for individual patients and staff and for institutions, and is likely to result in loss of utilitarian benefits.

CHERRI also recommends that a robust, simple-to-use and commonly acknowledged mechanism for handling consent with respect to clinical recordings is adopted across the UK. The CHERRI common consent and licensing model is proposed to address the problems. In alignment to the proposals of the CLIC project, it uses the simplicity of Creative Commons in seeking to accommodate specific clinical responsibilities and issues.

Meeting real needs

What all the projects agree on is that, if we are to provide any solution to the issues of digital image access, we really need to understand the needs, desires and objectives (and internal workflows) of genuine users, as well as their cultural limitations. This is perhaps best summed up in the Digital

Image Archiving study, which notes that the development of digital systems, like any non-digital system, should be led by an understanding of the needs of those people who will use them. The study gives great weight to what it terms end-users, but it also includes those who are engaged in digitising or creating born-digital images – the so-called start-users. In matters of preservation, as with all other elements of the digital world, the study acknowledges the need for any 'system' to adapt and grow in response to issues relating to change of use, copyright, wider accessibility and even metadata, within the communities that the system is designed to serve.

After debating the many and varied issues of preserving digital images, the Digital Image Archiving study makes a final point, that again confirms the findings of the other studies: that we need to work from a properly formed evidence base, regardless of the task in hand. We need more evidence of how people are using images, how they find them and how they manipulate them. The study also notes that we need to continue to share expertise and knowledge so that we build up a comprehensive knowledge and evidence base for the work we do, and so that we can place as much confidence in digital image repositories as we do in the galleries, libraries and archives that we trust with our non-digital heritage.

As suspected, the results of the commissioned studies have clearly demonstrated that a more community-led approach is necessary to meet the differing and complicated image needs of the HE and FE communities. The core of the IWG's vision is to respond to the *realities* of UK education, exploiting the benefits of technology and enabling image suppliers to achieve their own strategic aims, in order to meet the real needs of image users in teaching, learning and research.

Recommendations

The IWG recommends:

- a change of culture in the provision, access and use of digital images in education

- discussion of the creation of a managed service within the JISC Information Environment that supports a national network of digital images: a virtual reservoir

- clear lines for developing processes and facilities that enable organisations and individuals to interact in enhanced ways with the images of the virtual reservoir

- analysis of the tools and facilities that may be required to support the reservoir

- exploration of manageable elements of the needs of the art and cultural heritage sector, including decisions about control (or lack of control) of metadata/categorisation and licensing issues etc., in order to begin the process of creating a virtual reservoir

- identification of the mechanisms necessary to support the continued development, and ongoing maintenance, of the digital-image reservoir, including devolvement of responsibilities and levels of security/freedom

- discussion of how services (such as TASI[16], AHDS[17], EDINA[18] and MIMAS[19]) will support the reservoir, to what level and in what context; for example, will training be offered in digitisation, licensing etc., via the reservoir?

- consideration of how a virtual reservoir could evolve to cover all subject areas, and possibly other digital formats, across the UK and liaise with other national bodies (Museums Libraries Archives, national galleries etc.) as well as wider, European or international, initiatives and other image-centric organisations (e.g. Copyright Licensing Authority – CLA[20], and Design and Artists Copyright Society – DACS[21]).

JISC image activity – past to present

Over the past 11 years JISC has supported the provision of digital-image resources for FE and HE communities, primarily through wide-reaching and successful digitisation programmes and the licensing of a number of commercial image collections. Images were a specific programme area in the second phase of eLib, and 7% (£1,030,000) of eLib funding went to work in this area. The following list summarises some of the activities that the JISC has supported:

Higher Education Library for Image Exchange (HELIX)[22]. The HELIX image collection was created as a result of Elib funding granted in 1996. The HELIX project – based at De Montfort University – aimed to develop a substantial body of images to be based on distributed image banks held in the partner institutions. The service was launched in 1998 and hosted 52,200 JISC-funded or licensed images from various collections including Hulton Getty .

JISC Image Digitisation Initiative (JIDI)[23] and the Knowledge Gallery. The JIDI project provided a means of identifying, coordinating and monitoring the digitisation of 13 image collections, the digitisation of which was funded by JISC. Nine of these are hosted by AHDS Visual Arts (see below). JIDI was managed by the Institute for Learning and Research Technology at the University of Bristol.

Technical Advisory Service for Images (TASI). TASI was founded as a JISC Service in 1996, and continues to provide high-quality, essential services in support of digital-image creation, management and use.

Arts and Humanities Data Service (AHDS). The JISC has funded many image collections through AHDS Visual Arts[24] (formerly Visual Arts Data Service – VADS), via several digitisation programmes and, through part funding of the whole Arts and Humanities Data Service, provides access to some 100,000 digital images. AHDS was founded in 1996.

AMICO. The AMICO Art Library reflected an agreement between JISC and The Art Museum Image Consortium (AMICO) in 2001. The JISC provided AMICO a total payment of £400,000 for the content and to provide the service delivery over three years. As JISC recovered only £20,950 through institutional subscription, this was a highly subsidised collection with little take-up.

SCRAN[25]. The SCRAN Resource Base is an archive of over 300,000 copyright-cleared images. From November 2000 until October 2005 the JISC funded a national deal for this image collection which, after subscriptions are taken into account, amounted to a subsidy of £294,139 over five years.

PICTIVA[26]. The 2000-02 PICTIVA (Promoting the use of on-line Image Collections in Learning and Teaching In the Visual Arts) e-learning and tools project addressed problems affecting use of online resources. Outputs of the PICTIVA project have enriched the AHDS Visual Arts service.

PIXUS. The PIXUS demonstrator portal provided access to a number of collections, including SCRAN, AHDS – Visual Arts, Wellcome Trust, Resources for Learning in Scotland (RLS) and British Geological Survey.

Timeline for images work supported by JISC, 1996–2006

1995–	1996
- Electronic Libraries Programme (eLib) - DIGIMAP - Higher Education Library for Image Exchange (HELIX) - Medical Images: Digitised Reference Information Bank (MIDRIB)	- Technical Advisory Service for Images (TAS - Higher Education Digitisation Service (HED - Arts and Humanities Data Service (AHDS) - JISC Image Digitisation Initiative (JIDI)

Education Image Gallery (EIG)[27]. The EIG is an archive of 50,000 copyright-cleared images from the Getty Images collection. The previous JISC-subsidised licence ran until July 2007, achieving an efficiency gain to the education community of £1.8 million per year. JISC Collections has recently announced the new agreement that has been extended to include schools. An important aspect of the licence is that any images incorporated into printed learning and teaching materials can continue to be used even after the current sub-licence expires. Although EIG offers excellent value for money to institutions, the fact that it is not a user-led collection must be a contributing factor in the degree to which its use must be subsidised.

MIDESS[28]. The Management of Images in a Distributed Environment with Shared Services (MIDESS) project, JISC-funded for two years from June 2005, is exploring the management of digitised content in institutional and cross-institutional contexts through the development of a digital repository infrastructure. It is addressing how support can be provided for the use of digital content in a learning and research context, in an integrated manner. It will also explore how use and management of digital content can be joined up in a national context.

Art Museum Image Gallery[29]. The Art Museum Image Gallery is a collection of over 160,000 images from museums around the world. It is made available on subscription for educational use through JISC Collections from February 2007. Images of both fine and decorative arts are included and the initial agreement covers three years.

Image resources that JISC has funded directly are, clearly, more likely to remain available to the education community. However, over the last 11 years the JISC has invested a substantial sum in creating and licensing image collections for the academic community. Unfortunately, at that time, there were a number of hard-to-identify cultural issues/barriers associated with using these collections. As a consequence it has been difficult to secure sustainable (and economical) use. This problem has been, and continues to be, exacerbated by the fact that owners of (licensed) digital-image content

1996–1998	1999	1999–2000
▪ eLib Standards Guidelines, v.1.0, 2.0	▪ Resource Discovery Network (RDN) launched	▪ JISC Distributed Image Service scoped; agreed as JISC policy

Three figures beholding a Vision of the Heavenly City
© Albert Knox Art gallery, Buffalo, New York, Art Museum Image Gallery (AMIG).

have been unwilling to provide licences in perpetuity. This means it has not been possible for the JISC to build a long-term asset for its community or even to guarantee continuous access to image resources which lecturers, students and researchers have integrated into their work. Furthermore, although many images are now available to the education community, particularly since the advent of portal technologies, it is still hard to generate consistent usage. The vision accepts that many of the issues to do with digital image use are nebulous and hard to define, but hopes that, with a community-led approach, some of these issues will become identifiable, and thus solvable.

A framework for achieving the vision

In February 2005, the IWG met over two days to explore how the JISC might be able to provide its community with the most effective range of digital images, that would: meet general, specific and local teaching/learning/research needs; be sustainable and affordable; and provide the foundation for a long-term resource.

The result of the February brainstorming session was the vision for a virtual reservoir of digital images. To support the vision, the group identified

Timeline for images work supported by JISC, 1996–2006

2001	2002	2003	2004	2005
▪ Images Working Group (IWG) first meets ▪ AMICO Art Library and SCRAN Resource Base made available	▪ PICTIVA	▪ Images Working Group remit re-defined ▪ PIXUS demonstrator portal	▪ Education Image Gallery (EIG)	▪ National Vis for Images

several benefits that such a reservoir would provide for the UK HE and FE communities. It would:

- allow institutions to house their own digital image collections within their institutional or regional repositories and also be part of a national, virtual-reservoir network

- allow teachers and academics to deposit and access images created for educational purposes

- allow institutions to share image collections and provide users with continual online access

- provide the scaffolding for other public-sector image-collection owners to make their collections available to FE and HE, thereby providing extra depth to the reservoir

- promote the notion of sustainability through the perceived security of multiple partners, stakeholders and users

- create a critical mass of images with high relevance to education, ensuring healthy use of the service

- be an open-access service, enabling the community to feel a great sense of ownership

- comply with JISC standards ensuring interoperability and ease of access

- promote metadata standards to ensure easy resource discovery by the entire range of users in the community

- be designed to encourage use by all members of the community, particularly those identified as traditionally non-image-users

- encourage image quality standards as identified by the JISC IWG and JISC Services to support deposit, access and sharing of images

- maximise use of TASI, AHDS Visual Arts and other relevant services funded by the JISC as providers of advice on best practice and training

2005–2007	2006
• Management of Images in a Distributed Environment with Shared Services (MIDESS) • Visual and Sound Materials (VSM) media-specific portal demonstrator	• INTUTE launched as the new face of the RDN • the Digital Picture • Common Healthcare Educational Recordings Reusability Infrastructure (CHERRIE) • Community-Led Image Collections (CLIC) • Digital Images Archiving Study

- provide a straightforward avenue for the dissemination of JISC-funded images, resolving some of the issues relating to digitisation.

To achieve the vision, and develop these benefits, the IWG has devised a notional framework to enable coherent digital image collection development, management and use across UK FE and HE communities, in conjunction with the JISC's Information Environment.

Figure 1.1 outlines how digital images could, through utilising the facilities and services of the wider JISC IE, be drawn from multiple sources, fed through image-specific portals and accessed via specialist interfaces incorporated or pointing to whichever system is relevant to the user community.

Figure 1.1
The IWG's vision overlaid on the JISC Information Environment.

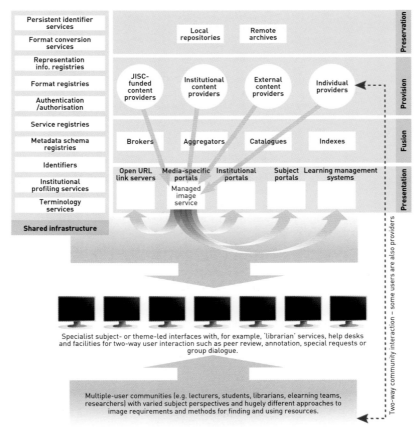

Digital Images in Education: Realising the Vision

The next chapter sets out the wider context of digital-image creation, use and management, looking beyond education and beyond the UK. Then the following four chapters detail the findings of the four recent digital-image reports summarised above. JISC Collections and the JISC Executive, in consultation with the IWG and the broader image-using UK tertiary education community, have planned – and in some cases already set in progress – initial steps toward realising the vision conceived by the Images Working Group. These activities are described in the final chapter of this book.

References

1. JISC Images Working Group (IWG)
    http://www.jisc-collections.ac.uk/workinggroups/images.aspx

2. JISC Collections
    http://www.jisc-collections.ac.uk/
    JISC Collections. From Wikipedia, the free encyclopedia
    http://en.wikipedia.org/wiki/JISC_Collections

3. JISC Collections Working Groups
    http://www.jisc-collections.ac.uk/workinggroups.aspx

4. JISC (Joint Information Systems Committee)
    http://www.jisc.ac.uk/

5. the Digital Picture
    See chapter 3. The full report is available online:
    http://thedigitalpicture.ac.uk/documents/pdf/digital_picture_final_report.pdf
    The project website:
    http://thedigitalpicture.ac.uk/home.html

6. CLIC: Community Led Image Collections – a study
    See chapter 4. The full report is available online:
    http://www.jisc.ac.uk/uploaded_documents/CLIC_Report.pdf
    The project website provides further information about collections:
    http://www.oucs.ox.ac.uk/ltg/projects/clic/

7. CHERRI (Common Healthcare Educational Recordings Reusability Infrastructure)
    See chapter 5. The full report is available online:
    http://www.cherri.mvm.ed.ac.uk/cherri.pdf
    The project website is:
    http://www.cherri.mvm.ed.ac.uk/

8. Digital Images Archiving Study
    See chapter 6. The full report is available online:
    http://www.jisc.ac.uk/uploaded_documents/FinaldraftImagesArchivingStudy.pdf

9. The Visual and Sound Materials portal scoping study and demonstrator project
    http://www.jisc.ac.uk/index.cfm?name=project_vsmportal

10. PIXUS Image Portal Demonstrator
http://www.jisc.ac.uk/whatwedo/programmes/programme_portals/project_
image_portal.aspx

11. JISC Core Theme: Information Environment
http://www.jisc.ac.uk/whatwedo/themes/information_environment.aspx

12. JISC Core Theme: e-Learning
http://www.jisc.ac.uk/whatwedo/themes/elearning.aspx

13. JISC Digital Repositories Programme
http://www.jisc.ac.uk/whatwedo/programmes/programme_digital_
repositories.aspx

14. Jorum – helping to build a community for sharing
http://www.jorum.ac.uk/

15. Creative Commons
http://creativecommons.org/

16. Technical Advisory Service for Images (TASI)
http://www.tasi.ac.uk/

17. AHDS (Arts and Humanities Data Service)
http://ahds.ac.uk/

18. EDINA – providing national online resources for education and research
http://edina.ac.uk/

19. MIMAS (Manchester Information and Associated Services)
http://www.mimas.ac.uk

20. CLA (Copyright Licensing Agency)
http://www.cla.co.uk/

21. DACS (Design and Artists Copyright Society)
http://www.dacs.org.uk/

22. HELIX Case Study. TASI Case Studies of Digitisation Projects
http://www.tasi.ac.uk/resources/helix.html

23. JISC's Image Digitisation Initiative (JIDI) Case Study. TASI Case Studies of
Digitisation Projects
http://www.tasi.ac.uk/resources/jidi.html

24. AHDS Visual Arts
http://ahds.ac.uk/visualarts/

25. SCRAN
http://www.scran.ac.uk/

26. PICTIVA project. AHDS Visual Arts
http://vads.ahds.ac.uk/learning/pictiva/

27. EIG (Education Image Gallery)
Login:
http://edina.ac.uk/eig/
Description:
http://www.jisc-collections.ac.uk/eig
Full product description in JISC Collections Catalogue of online resources:
http://www.jisc-collections.ac.uk/catalogue/coll_educationimagegallery/eig_productdescription.aspx

28. MIDESS (Management of Images in a Distributed Environment with Shared Services)
http://www.leeds.ac.uk/library/midess/index.html

29. Art Museum Image Gallery
http://www.jisc-collections.ac.uk/catalogue/coll_amig.aspx/

Chapter 2

The Digital Image Landscape

Leona Carpenter with Catherine Draycott and Stuart Dempster

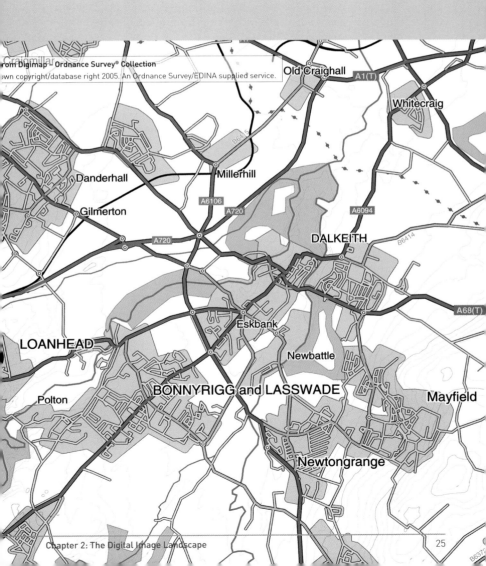

The vision set out by the Images Working Group was developed, and will be realised, within the context of the broader landscape of digital image creation, use and management. This landscape can be mapped to take in education, but also libraries, museums and archives, and in particular the picture libraries of these organisations; public-sector education, libraries, museums and archives, but also commercial organisations, and collaborations among public-sector and commercial organisations; the United Kingdom, but also European, Australian and North American initiatives. Much of the focus for academic content creation, collection, use, sharing for re-use, and preservation has been on peer-reviewed research reports, research data and, more recently, items classified as learning objects. Digital images may occur within any of these categories, in addition to constituting an educational and research resource category in their own right. However – as the vision for the future and the studies reported here make clear – as well as having tremendous potential for enriching the experience of learners and enhancing many areas of research, digital images do present challenges that are different from or more severe than those for other resource types. Digital images arise from a multiplicity of sources, are put to a multiplicity of uses, have high levels of complexity of copyright and format issues, and consequently present exceptional challenges for discovery, use and curation.

Multiplicity of sources and uses

Digitisation

Digitisation projects and programmes have been seen as the main source of digital images useful in UK post-16 education. While many of these resources are produced within the public sector, some have been purchased or licensed for use from commercial providers or the commercial units of public-sector organisations. At time of writing, JISC has a major digitisation programme in hand – as described in the final chapter of this book – which will naturally result in the creation of many digital images. (Past JISC-supported digitisation projects were discussed in the previous chapter.) Although the remit of the digitisation programme is broader than simply to produce images, images will undoubtedly feature significantly in projects funded within it.

Funding sources beyond JISC have been and continue to be made available for initiatives involving digitisation. Many cultural-heritage organisations such as national and specialist museums and the British Library[1] have embarked on major digitisation programmes in order to enhance access to their collections, as well as to support collection management and to generate income from sales or licensing of image reproduction rights to publishers.

A post-war combine harvester

© The Museum of English Rural Life.

Tory Stewart Farm, Blandford, 21 June 1937

© The Museum of English Rural Life.

Film digitisation – for example from British Pathe[2], with twelve million still images at the time of writing – provides a rich source for digital images. Further images are being captured as part of programmes of digitisation of archival texts such as newspaper digitisation by the British Library[3], and by newspaper companies themselves. Less obvious sources for digitisation have also provided rich resources for the academic community. Reading University's Museum of English Rural Life *Farmer and Stockbreeder* and *Farmers Weekly*[4] magazine glass-plate photographic negative collection is an example, with samples of the digitised images available as an online exhibition[5].

Born-digital images, social computing and Web 2.0

Digitisation of existing images is now perhaps taking a back seat to the capture or creation of original digital images as a major source. This is importantly, but far from solely, the case in certain areas of scientific research such as chemistry and astrophysics, where images are core research data. Microscopy and other instrument-based data-gathering techniques generate enormous quantities of digital images, images that could be re-used in many areas of research and in learning and teaching. The overlapping categories of students, lecturers, researchers and artists are creating digital still and moving images using solely digital tools. The growth in this activity has been accelerated by the increasingly affordable availability of near-professional quality digital cameras, many of which are sold accompanied by relatively easy-to-use image-manipulation software applications such as Photoshop Elements (Adobe)[6,7] and GIMP (open source)[8]. Much professional photography is now digital in origin, bypassing the need for wet processing and later digitisation. In addition to photography, the education community is becoming increasingly confident in its ability to create graphic images through digital means, whether using specialist software applications or the simpler utilities built into office productivity packages such as Microsoft Office.

Image creation has thus ceased to be the preserve of photographic and design professionals. Digital images are being created by everyone and anyone, a development that echoes the proliferation of small-scale publishing efforts enabled a generation ago by the advent of desk-top publishing. Technology is increasingly seen as an enabler, rather than a driver of intensified activity in this area, with 'user-created content' starting to have importance for many news and entertainment sectors, as well as for education, and with many grass-roots creators eager to share their images. For example, see *Your news, your pictures*[9, 10] for the BBC News invitation to its audience to contribute pictures and short video clips on breaking news stories and *'... visual interpretation of both local and global issues as well as just great pictures of your daily lives'*, and for links to user-created content. (Note that VJ is an acronym that may mean either video journalism or providing visual backgrounds for music. For the latter, sometimes referred to as VJing, see BBC-VJ[11].)

Creating and sharing an immediate visual response to momentous events has relevance not only for news reporting, but also for educational use and eventually as academic source documents, becoming part of the evidence base for domains such as history and social science. The Flickr pool of photographs relating to the bombings in London on 7 July 2005 is one such resource. There are many such event- or theme-based 'pools' in Flickr[12], a web-based application for storing, sharing, organising and finding your own photos, as well as finding and commenting on the photos of others. Access to your photos can be limited to specified groups of friends and family, or contributed to subject- or event-based groups.

Falling somewhere between commercial provision and community or social computing are image sharing and sales facilities such as deviantART[13]. Many subscribers to deviantArt are offering versions of their works for sale in non-digital forms from photographic prints to mugs and fridge magnets, while making digital versions available for downloading without charge; other subscribers seem interested only in showing or sharing their images for discussion and/or downloading .

Although initiatives such as Flickr and MySpace[14] (the social-networking website) are often categorised as Web 2.0 applications, they might more usefully be thought of as community or social computing applications. Although the business models for such enterprises rely on the generation of an income stream from advertising, possibly supplemented by subscription income for access to enhanced features and/or relief from advertisements, the mainstay of the business models is what might be termed the gift economy. Unless hundreds of thousands of members contribute content free of charge, there will be insufficient traffic for advertisers to take an interest. It is important to note that while these initiatives are usually independent start-ups, the successful ones are often bought up by large companies. Flickr is now owned by Yahoo!, and MySpace is part of News Corporation, the Rupert Murdoch media conglomerate. The studies reported in this book shed much light on academic community-based digital image creation and community-led image collecting and sharing of collections, and explore the potential of social computing for academic creators, collectors and users of digital images.

Uses for learning and teaching

Two of the studies reported in this book look in detail at domains where the use of digital images is particularly crucial for learning and teaching – clinical images and the arts. However, it is clear that images are important resources across most post-16 education. Much of the usage observed across all of the studies was relatively simple, illustrative use. While the value of such use must not be underestimated, as more and more learners – and those who teach them – come to view the use of computers and digital resources as a normal part of their educational experience, more innovative uses of images are certain to become prevalent, and new uses will continue to emerge. For examples of the kinds of tools that are becoming familiar to the school children who will be tomorrow's university students, see Enquiring Minds' selection of digital tools for education[15], one of which is the digital camera.

Image-based collaborative art is one emerging area of image use, where *Image Matter*, a collaboration by Dave Kemp and Kevin Robbie, is an interesting cross-disciplinary project.[16] Kemp is a visual artist, Robbie a physicist specialising in nanostructured materials; they base their work on advances in digital technologies related to photographic images. The artist encourages the onward use of the resulting new images. Collaborations of this kind are being developed by art and design researchers and students, including those led by Alison Dalwood[17] and others at the University of Herefordshire Centre for Research in Electronic Art and Communication (CREAC), where *Field of Vision*[18], a live art collaborative project has had physical site-based exhibitions in the UK, USA, Germany, China and elsewhere.

> *The use of the internet was explored by Stephan Klimas, Alison Dalwood and Michael Wright through the collaboration in Digital arts projects entitled 'Field of Vision'. The concept of this work is to utilise the web to call for submissions of imagery based on thematic concepts and attitudes. These submissions are organised both in a site-based installation and as a web-based site. The research exploits the use of the internet as a tool for collecting both idiosyncratic and collective attitudes in the form of imagery and addresses questions of aesthetic and conceptual organisation of collective imagery.*
> **Michael Wright, Sept 05[19]**

Image Matter, Joseph Philibert Girault, Athenes 1842...
© Dave Kemp and Kevin Robbie.

Uses for research

As mentioned earlier, a number of scientific domains rely particularly heavily on images as research data. In some cases, these data are generated in such massive quantities as to provide drivers for technical development and collaborative initiatives for their use. An example is Media Grid[20, 21], which is providing a software development (computational grid) platform for handling massive quantities of digital media such as real-time visualisation of complex weather patterns. Other innovative research uses of images abound. Through an online game, Peekaboom[22] gathers information about random images on the web and then uses this information to train computer vision algorithms.

Outside science, technology and medicine, areas of interest include brush-stroke level forensic examination of works of art across a number of paintings distributed among geographically distant collections using high-resolution digital images. And, of course, access to digital images of collection items is also helpful in preparing to get the most out of visits to the collections themselves, an activity relevant both to research and to learning and teaching. Forensic examination of archival texts through digital imaging has also proved useful in the humanities, social sciences and historic research. An early example of such examination is the *Electronic Beowulf*[23, 24] which showed how effective then-new technologies can be in exploring ancient materials, when allied with detailed scholarly research.

User needs studies

Have user needs relating to images been adequately identified? Diane Harley and her colleagues at the Center for Studies in Higher Education, University of California, Berkeley, conclude in a study on humanities and social science usage of digital resources[25] that there are a number of challenges in studying users and usage, but important reasons for finding ways to do so. Not least are the aims of improving tools and services for users and as an input into investment decisions. The studies reported in this book are helping to take us forward in relation to a user focus, while suggesting that much remains to be done. For example, section four of the full project report of the Community-Led Image Collections (CLIC) study outlines an analysis of image users' and providers' needs, based in part on *the* Digital Picture survey results.

Complexity of copyright, licensing and format

The Images Working Group's vision draws attention to issues of copyright and licensing for sustainable collections of digital images for use in education and research. Chapters three, four, five and six reporting the studies and chapter seven on the way forward to realising the vision discuss in some detail these issues and how they might be addressed. Here we simply highlight some of the issues, and some initiatives in the broader landscape that attempt to address them. As is brought out time and again, copyright in digital images can be extremely complex. This is especially the case where the source of the image is a photograph. Permission clearance may involve a combination of any of (for example):

- a photographer
- a later manipulator of the original image
- a commissioner of the image
- an organisation that employed the photographer or image manipulator

- the licensor of a software tool required to interpret and display the image

- a creator of an object that appears in the image

- any identifiable person who appears in the image

- the creator or owner of any metadata attached to the images

In the biological sciences, an example of community-based image collection whose use has been embraced by academics is the Bioscience ImageBank[26], [27], with images contributed by academics, researchers, learned societies, industry and individuals, and managed by the Higher Education Academy Centre for Bioscience. It could be argued that the success of this jointly funded HE Academy and JISC initiative is in large part due to the clarity of the copyright status of the images provided. The British Academy has produced useful guidelines relating to copyright issues for research in the humanities and social sciences.[28] These guidelines on the application of copyright in the context of the work of academic researchers include sections on situations relating to image reproduction and to still images captured from moving-image sources.

Creative Commons

The Creative Commons[29] initiative is widely acknowledged as offering creators choices in the way rights in their creations are apportioned. Since its inception in December 2002, it has become increasingly influential. The ability to apply a choice of forms of Creative Commons licences is built in to some of the social computing services, such as Flickr, described above. While it may not be directly applicable in all areas of academic image-collection sharing, the models implicit in the Creative Commons licensing procedures are at least relevant. The Creative Commons logo attached to an image provides linkage to clear information about the rights in that image – what you are and are not allowed to do with it, and under what circumstances – and is increasingly widely recognised as doing so. The Creative Commons web site also provides links to sites providing images under Creative Commons licences.[30] Creative Commons UK[31] provides licences tailored to the three separate UK jurisdictions of England, Scotland and Wales, and links to featured UK content available under Creative Commons licences.

Gowers Review

As part of the Pre-Budget Report 2005 package, the Chancellor of the Exchequer asked Andrew Gowers to lead an independent review to examine the UK's intellectual property rights (IPR) framework. The outcome of the review could lead to a revision of copyright law in relation to images, as well as many other forms of intellectual-property-related legislation. There were many responses to the Gowers Review of Intellectual Property Call for Evidence, which closed on 21 April 2006. In addition to the JISC response, TASI (Technical Advisory Service for Images) provided a full and detailed response to the review.[32]

Based on an analysis of all these submissions and a wide range of other evidence, the Final Report of the Gowers Review was published in early December 2006 and posted on the HM Treasury web site.[33] It includes a number of recommendations which will support greater use of a variety of material (including digital images) for teaching and learning, and ease the legal challenges to preserving such material for future use. Recommendation 2 would improve the balance of legislative instruments by enabling educational provisions to cover distance learning and interactive whiteboards. Recommendations 8 and 9 would improve the flexibility of instruments through introducing a limited private copying exception for format shifting and through extending private copying for research to cover all forms of content. Recommendations 10a and 10b would improve flexibility through enabling archival copying and format shifting of archival copies by libraries. Recommendation 11 is that a European copyright harmonisation directive (Directive 2001/29/EC) be amended to allow for creative, transformative or derivative works, as long as they do not conflict with a normal exploitation of the work and do not unreasonably prejudice the legitimate interests of the rights holder. Recommendation 12 is to create an exception to copyright for the purpose of caricature, parody or pastiche.

Also relevant are recommendations 13, 14a and 14b, the implementation of which would clarify the meaning of 'reasonable search' and legal liability in the tracing of ownership of works for which the copyright owner is unknown – commonly known as 'orphan works' – thus facilitating the use of such works. Overall, the Final Report underlines the need for balance and flexibility in intellectual property legislation, and acknowledges the importance of access to resources for education and research, which is severely limited under current legislation.

Moral Rights

A further area of rights complexity of particular relevance to the use of digital images in education is the area of Moral Rights, which promote respect for the quality of a creation and recognition of role of the creator. Moral Rights cannot be assigned, although they can be waived. Naomi Korn[34] sets out these issues clearly in the Minerva *Guide to Intellectual Property Rights and Other Legal Issues*.[35] As she points out, the moral right to object through the courts to derogatory treatment *'is an important right to observe when reproducing digital images. If images are altered or manipulated, shown in detail or reproduced in a way other than fully without the rights holder consent, this could be viewed as derogatory treatment.'* As well as the right to object to derogatory treatment, Moral Rights include the right to be identified as the author, the right to object to false attribution and the right to privacy in films and photographs.

Format complexity

Perhaps the most challenging technical issue for the management of digital image collections is the level of complexity relating to formats. As explained in some detail by the Technical Advisory Service for Images (TASI), digital images may be created and stored in a range of different file formats, each developed to meet a different set of needs.[36, 37] This does provide for desirable flexibility, but also contributes to the challenges for use and preservation of images, and for interoperability among systems. In addition, although formats may have the status of standards, there can be local variations of format specifications as well as the variations inherent in the evolution of format specifications over time. This area of complexity is just one of the reasons that TASI is so important for UK post-16 education as a feature of the digital-image landscape.

Challenges for discovery and curation

Retrieval methods and metadata for discovery

Describing images in ways that are useful for their retrieval by a range of users with very different requirements for their use has been a challenge since the first days of picture libraries. It could be said that the 'meaning' of a picture is in the eye of the beholder. Descriptive cataloguing of images has traditionally been costly and less effective than desired, with many picture researchers simply relying on visual scans through large and perhaps broadly categorised sets of reduced-size versions of images. More recently, attempts to reduce costs and improve retrieval results have focused on content-based retrieval, community annotation and social tagging, and computer vision experiments. For example, IMKA (Intelligent Multimedia Knowledge Application)[38] is a project that integrates a number of approaches.

The Andromeda Galaxy
© NASA, Robert Gendler (robgendlerastropixs.com).

Content-based image retrieval (CBIR) uses features such as shape, texture and colour as search parameters, by enabling the searcher to choose features from 'palettes', choose an image that is similar in some ways to the desired image, present an existing image or make a sketch for rough matching.[39, 40, 41] JISC funded a report on progress in CBIR as long ago as 1999 (Eakins and Graham[42]), and much more research in this area has been carried out since then. This is driven to some extent by its potential in supporting criminal investigation and anti-terrorism techniques – for an example of security-related applications, see Virage[43]. The EU-funded Artiste (an integrated art analysis and navigation environment)[44, 45, 46, 47] and Sculpteur (Semantic and content-based multimedia exploitation for European benefit)[48] projects investigated and demonstrated the possibilities of CBIR in the image collections of art galleries distributed across Europe, including the Uffizi in Florence, the National Gallery and the Victoria and Albert Museum in London, and the Centre de Recherche et de Restauration des Musées de France, the restoration centre for French museums, including the Louvre. Artiste ended in 2002 and Sculpteur, which followed it, ended in 2005.

The University of Southampton IT Innovation Centre[49] was a participant in both projects, and reports from both projects can be accessed through the Centre's web site. imgSeek[50] is an open-source application to try in this area, as it has a similarity-based (query-by-example) search facility, in addition to the more usual search options, where the query input can be either a rough sketch or an existing image. In the Sculpteur project, imgSeek was used on a test set of images to demonstrate some of the content-based retrieval.[51] imgSeek is available in versions for the Windows, Linux and Mac OS X platforms, under the Gnu Public License [sic] version 2.[52] INTUTE's May 2006 review of image search engines, while emphasising the experimental nature of content-based search engines, cites as examples the WebSEEk[53] project at Columbia University, Query by Image Content (QBICTM)[54] from IBM, the AHDS Visual Arts[55] collection and the IMAGINE[56] collection (Images, Museums and Galleries in the North East, funded by the Big Lottery Fund), and recommends the Wikipedia entry on CBIR.[57]

One of the advantages claimed for CBIR is that the features against which queries are matched can ordinarily be automatically extracted, rather than based on human work to create metadata. Community annotation and social tagging are alternatives to formal metadata creation and automatic discovery metadata extraction that have been actively explored over the past few years. In social computing applications, annotations may usually be added by image creators or by any other member of the community, often without any editorial function clearing function. They may be personal responses or may add textual information. Tags are essentially descriptor labels, with an interesting recent development being quite sophisticated facilities for geo-tagging to support search by place as an attribute of an image.[58, 59] Additional annotations may be text comments or some form of selection as favourites. These techniques are not applicable to images alone, of course. In del.icio.us, the social bookmarking web application, tags are words used to describe web bookmarks. The resource being bookmarked and tagged may be an image, and Flickr offers the option of saving pages to del.icio.us bookmarks.[60]

The ESP Game[61], developed at Carnegie-Mellon University and funded in part by the National Science Foundation (NSF), is helping to label all the images on the web – there are perhaps tens of billions of them – by showing anonymously-paired online players a selection of images that have been randomly pulled off the web. The object of the game-play is to make as many matches as possible by typing lots of relevant key words into the box provided to describe the image. Making a match moves the pair on to the next image and improves their scores. The aim is to use the results that are built up through playing the game to help provide much more accurate image searching, improve the accessibility of the web for the visually impaired, and help users block inappropriate images from their computers. There are some refinements beyond this simple description of the game, but they enhance rather than retard both game-play and results, and the game appears to attract a steady stream of players. Late in 2006, Phetch[62], a further image-description game from Carnegie-Mellon in which one player is a describer while another attempts to find the described image on the web, was in beta testing.

More science-fiction-like possibilities are on the horizon. Lakshmi Sandhana in 'This is a computer on your brain'[63] describes a new brain-computer-interface technology that could enable people to search through images ten times faster than human capacity will allow. Working under DARPA funding, researchers at Columbia University have developed the C3 Vision – a cortically coupled computer vision system – to make it easier to rapidly process hours of video footage by ranking images according to the neural signatures the brain emits as users comb through video footage or streaming images. The system taps into the ability of the brain to recognize an image far more quickly than the person can identify it. Although developed specifically for examining video and streams of images for crime-detection purposes, it is easy to see how the technology could be applied to image retrieval across large sets of images.

Meanwhile – at least until and unless some of the research and early practice in content-based retrieval, automatic metadata extraction and community annotation and social tagging develops into proven, established practice – it can be argued that expert creation of discovery metadata is one of the essential ways that managed image collections provide value to users. In support of this, TASI provides an introduction to the use of thesauri, classifications and authority lists for this purpose, and a list of those deemed particularly useful for describing images.[64]

Retrieval 'places' – the fragmentation of access routes

Where do you go when you want to find a digital image for some specific purpose? It may vary not only depending on your purpose, but also on your role within an organisation and your knowledge of the field of possibilities open to you. The BUBL Link Catalogue of Internet Resources[65] lists 161 image collections, some of which are themselves indexes of image or graphical resources available via the internet. In the JISC Collections catalogue of online resources some entries are for resources dedicated to digital images, such as the Education Image Gallery, the Satellite Image Data Service, Digimap – Ordnance Survey Collection and the Visual Arts Data Service. Other listed resources, such as Early English Books Online and SCRAN Resource, are also rich in images. The European Library (TEL)[66] offers an image search, via an advanced search option for type=image. In addition to the search services offered by individual commercial picture libraries, there are search services that search across picture library services, and even searches across the offerings of individual digital-image creators including digital artists and professional photographers.

BUBL, JISC Collections and TEL are among the many search destinations where selection and quality-control processes have been applied. However, almost every general search service – not only Google – also offers a specialised image-search facility. A further array of retrieval 'places' are offered by social-computing, Web 2.0-type, image-sharing initiatives such as Flickr. Then there are the image cross-search services that search across a range of other search services...

A CLIC report appendix compiled by Karla Youngs and Grant Young of TASI sets out in detail an examination of about 70 commercial image collections. The British Association of Picture Libraries and Agencies (BAPLA)[67] is the trade association representing most commercial picture libraries and picture agencies in the UK, as well as picture libraries of some organisations that do not consider themselves to be engaging in commercial activities. BAPLA provides information about finding, buying and selling images, thus providing a further path for image retrieval, in addition to the separate finding services provided by individual members. Many cultural-heritage-sector libraries and museums, mostly through their picture libraries, are members. (Note that picture libraries are often seen as part of the commercial arms of libraries, museums and archives.) BAPLA members collectively can supply more than 350 million images, although these images are not all held in digital formats. In 2006, as many as 42% of BAPLA members had only 20% of their collections digitised.

Fragmentation of access routes to images is a problem recognised by the IWG and highlighted in the JISC-funded studies reported in this book. In particular, see the detailed discussions in chapters three and four and in the full Digital Picture and CLIC reports on the number of image collections that exist within institutions providing post-16 education in the UK. The JISC Visual and Sound Materials (VSM)[68] portal feasibility and demonstrator project may offer part of the solution to the problem of fragmentation, as is explained in chapter seven. Recognition of the problems posed by fragmentation of access routes is widespread, and combating fragmentation was one of the motives for the EU funding of the eChase public-private collaborative project outlined below.

Managing digital image collections from creation to preservation

Challenges for curation across academic digital-image collections are identified in detail in the AHDS-led[69] study summarised in chapter six. It is worth noting here that good practice emerging in fields such as chemistry, astronomy and astrophysics can provide exemplars for developing practice in other domains. Looking to initiatives beyond the education and research communities, BAPLA has been discussing the development of a collecting model for picture libraries. There is a trend for private-sector picture libraries to have as much 'wholly-owned' material as possible. This is achieved through buying the copyright from the photographers, and has led to picture libraries being able to commission original photography, which – after the exclusivity period contracted to the original client – can be made available through other business models. Rights-managed, royalty-free, pay-per-view and subscriptions are different rights models offered by picture libraries for the academic community.

As well as engaging in marketing and lobbying activities, and organising events such as the Picture Buyers' Fair, BAPLA promotes best practice and participates in the development of industry standards. For commercial picture libraries, the necessity for dealing with standards issues in collection management is commercially driven, and may be seen as largely having been sorted out. This includes metadata standards, how to encode and where to keep metadata so that it is tightly linked to the described images. Nevertheless, formats and digital-preservation issues are constantly under discussion, best practice is robustly advocated and the issues of best practice for watermarking and ensuring that provenance metadata is (and remains) in some way attached to any individual image to which it applies remain to be resolved. BAPLA is participating in the Metadata Image Library Exploitation (MILE)[70] project funded under the EU *eContentplus* programme.[71] MILE focuses on metadata classification, metadata search and retrieval, and how to handle IPR and copyright metadata.

The main standards for supply of images by commercial picture libraries are the pic4press guidelines for the use of digital images. pic4press guidelines[72] are produced by the Periodical Publishers' Association (PPA), BAPLA and the Association of Photographers (AOP) to define how a photographer, agency or library should submit their imagery with the aim of providing confidence within the publication workflow. The current version of the pic4press guidelines is Version 2, with Version 3 due for launch in May 2007. National Occupational Standards (NOS) in Photo Imaging and Photo Processing,[73] produced by Skillset – based on incremental review of the 2002 version developed by the Photo Imaging NTO (National Training Organisation) – are expected to be published sometime early in 2007. (Skillset is the Sector Skills Council for the Audio Visual Industries.) These standards describe the skills, knowledge and understanding needed to perform the main roles and responsibilities for occupations within the photo-imaging sector. The standards will influence curriculum development for training courses for qualifications in these occupations.

Naturally, many initiatives that have a broader focus than images are nevertheless potentially very relevant to the management of digital image collections. An example is the EU co-funded PLANETS[74] project, which brings together key national libraries and national archives, as well as leading research institutes and technology vendors, in order to deliver a sustainable framework that will enable long-term preservation of digital content, increasing Europe's ability to ensure long-term access to its cultural and scientific heritage. Within the PLANETS project, the Testbed sub-project aims to:

- provide an infrastructure for testing and evaluating preservation action (e.g. migration, emulation) and characterisation tools and services, and to assist the validation of the effectiveness of different digital-preservation plans;

- provide an infrastructure for experimentation for the whole preservation community and thereby spur the development in the field of digital preservation;

- facilitate organisations to validate their digital-preservation plans against the PLANETS service infrastructure.

Coalitions of the willing – collaboration among organisations and across sectors

The challenges in serving the needs of stakeholders in image collections cannot efficiently be addressed by individual organisations, sectors or even wholly within individual nations. Major benefits of organisations working together include improved access through sharing images and improved return on investment through pooling of research and development resources. Although the vision set out in this book rightly focuses on the UK post-16 education sector and the importance of sharing among community-led collections and initiatives, the possibilities for and utility of collaborations beyond that sector and beyond the UK must be acknowledged. Examples of useful collaborative initiatives such as ARKive[75] and the PictureAustralia[76] work with Flickr[77] demonstrate the validity of this proposition.

ARKive is provided by the UK-based educational charity Wildscreen. It has more than 15,000 still images online, covering British flora and fauna as well as endangered species from around the world. In addition to photographic images, it holds video, audio, maps and text related to animal, plant, fungi and habitat biodiversity. ARKive was chosen as the *Sunday Times'* website of the year in 2006, and has also been a Sage Business Awards prize-winner. Its excellence is supported by contributions from broadcasting organisations including the BBC's Natural History Unit, whose former head proposed the original vision for ARKive. In 2001-2002 an associated project with ILRT[78] (Institute for Learning and Research Technology) at the University of Bristol was funded by Hewlett-Packard Labs. ARKive-ERA investigated the educational and functional issues surrounding the design, development and use of internet-based, large multimedia database systems to support learning and teaching.[79, 80]

PictureAustralia provides one of the best examples of a cultural-heritage-sector service built upon a collaboration among agencies and enriched through a further collaboration with the public at large as content providers through the use of Flickr. While many of the over 40 cultural agencies (libraries, galleries, museums and archives) participating may be partially motivated by the desire to sell reproduction rights, the major outcome of the initiative is increasing awareness of and audiences for the content of their collections. The service provides access to more than one million images, and by extending the collaboration to the public at large, by autumn of 2006 over 9,000 images had been added to PictureAustralia. Enabling the public to contribute has added many contemporary images to the service, as well as enriching the heritage image collections. Although most Flickr-contributed images are available only through links to the Flickr site, some are selected for collection and preservation by the National Library of Australia[81]. Additional information about how this works is available through the library's website – see especially the staff paper by Judith Pearce.[82]

Fiona Hooton, the National Library of Australia's manager of PictureAustralia, in an evaluative article in *Gateways*, says that in addition to 'helping PictureAustralia to capture both past and present reflections of Australia and its people ... [that] enables political and social analysis of the impact of past and contemporary themes on Australian culture and daily life... [the PictureAustralia-Flickr pilot] project has made crucial links between media, culture and technology'.[83] Lorcan Dempsey has praised the project for *'putting the library in the flow of users'*: one of the reasons for choosing to collaborate with Flickr was that many Australians were already members of Flickr. In addition, through encouraging tagging, Flickr was supporting the creation of discovery metadata, and it seemed that its programming interface could easily be mapped to Dublin Core, already in use in contributing records to PictureAustralia.[84] The PictureAustralia service grew out of a much smaller collaborative project among only a handful of albeit major agencies initiated in 1998 and acknowledges the inspiration of a number of UK initiatives, including Helix, SCRAN[85] and TASI.

Many stakeholders acknowledge the importance of **public-commercial sector partnerships**, which attempt to steer a course between profit-making and public-good motivations. Although there are very many picture libraries around the world – BAPLA alone has 400 members – some organisations are large enough to play a dominant role. CORBIS[86] and Getty Images[87] are examples of such 'big players', perhaps large enough to make academic institutions cautious about participating in collaborative projects in which one of them is involved. Nevertheless, many such initiatives are underway, including eChase.

eChase (electronic Cultural Heritage made Accessible for Sustainable Exploitation)[88], a project funded under the now-closed European Commission eContent programme (European Digital Content on the global networks), '... seeks to demonstrate that public-private partnerships between content holders and commercial service providers can create new services and a sustainable business based on access and exploitation of digital cultural-heritage content at a European level'. Partners include Getty Images and Southampton University's IT Innovation Centre and Intelligence, Agents, Multimedia (IAM) Group. Under the umbrella of its broader objectives, eChase could contribute to the improvement of access to multimedia collections, particularly picture libraries and archives, by integrating metadata from different sites and producing semantic web interfaces. The **eContent Programme** covering the period 2001-2004 was followed by the **eContentplus** Programme, which aims to support the development of multilingual content for innovative, online services across the EU. The four-year programme (2005-2008), with a budget of €149 million to tackle the fragmentation of the European digital content market and improve the accessibility and usability of geographical information, cultural content and educational material, is likely to cover a number of activities with relevance to image collections.

Of course, commercial organisations other than picture libraries may participate in such projects, as in the PLANETS project described above. Partners in PLANET include four technology companies, in addition to libraries, archives and universities. The incentives for commercial organisations to participate include **benefiting from the funding of metadata enhancement, research co-funding, increasing the market for their products and services, and perhaps even digitisation funding**. On the other hand, some commercial organisations may help to fund the digitisation of resources held by cultural-heritage sector organisations in return for the right to engage in commercial exploitation of the resulting images. All stakeholders can benefit from collaboration to **improve interoperability** through, for example, agreements on DTDs (Document Type Definitions) that will support services such as aggregated access through a portal. Sharing development of standards and processes for image-collection management is another area where collaboration can improve interoperability.

Access management is another area where challenges can only be met through collaboration. Not only academic institutions, but also picture libraries and publishers see value in services such as Athens[89] and the newer Shibboleth that enable access over networks, but support restricted or managed use, rather than simply putting things in the public domain. In this way they can feel confident in adopting emerging models such as 'open content alliance'.[90,91] The UK Access Management Federation[92] uses Shibboleth[93], a standards-based application that has gained wide international acceptance as a common framework for access management. Membership of the Federation is open to all educational and research organisations (along with certain other publicly-funded bodies) and any commercial organisation providing services to the education and research sectors. JISC and BECTA (the British Educational Communication and Technology Agency)[94] support the Federation, which is operated by JANET UK .[95] Access to the Education Image Gallery is managed through the Federation and also through the Athens authentication service. Many image resources, ARTstor[96] for example, use Athens to manage access. Through the Federation, Shibboleth offers further advantages for access management, including international standardisation and more granular access control. JISC funds Eduserv to provide inter-working between Shibboleth and Athens sites through federated gateways.[97]

Access management is appropriate not only for subscription-based access models and where IPR must be protected, but also in cases where security, confidentially or privacy are at issue, and where access is restricted to communities that share certain resources. For example, access to some medical images may be restricted to a particular group of medical practitioners. Access management may also be used in conjunction with usage tracking. Collection owners want to keep track of the use of their images for a variety of reasons. Managing rights is also about tracking **usage outcomes** for learning and dissemination and indicating what resources to prioritise for digitisation or creation – what people use giving some indication, at least, of what they need. Usage patterns can support and validate planning and spending processes and decisions. Access-management processes also support ways of assuring the **authenticity** and **provenance** of images. Processes that support this assurance are seen as important elements of the value added by picture libraries. It is partly for this reason that a picture library-type access-management model has been adopted by many organisations in the cultural-heritage sector.[98,99]

A landscape in tension?

It has become apparent from this brief survey of the digital image landscape that there are a number of features that could produce conflict. There are those who argue that sustainability can only be achieved through commerce that enables creators and collection managers to 'make a living', while others maintain that sustainability must be built on collegiality and the gift economy. Global players (whether in the commercial or public sectors) may be seen as in competition with or alternatives to local, more community-based collections. However, these can more properly be seen as creative tensions, capable of generating the solutions needed to resolve them. Creative Commons licensing is one such tension-generated solution, while JORUM[100] and other learning-object repositories provide further examples.

A conference hosted by the Museums Copyright Group[101] in association with Kings College London, Connecting Culture and Commerce: Getting the Right Balance, was held in January 2007 at the National Gallery.[102] Decision makers from the museum, library, archive and education communities came together with those from the creative industries, media, legal, commerce and other business sectors to explore ways of opening wider public access

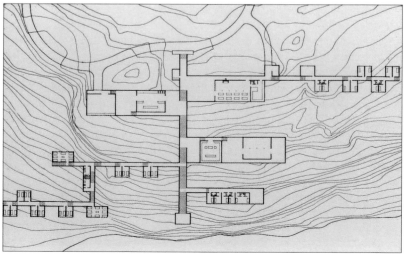

E L Barnes Architectural Drawing
© E L Barnes, via Pidgeon Digital.

to their collections, balanced against the needs to protect rights. Discussion focussed on emerging business and licensing models and their legislative framework, as well as technological change and the opportunities and challenges that it presents for new working practices and partnerships. The conference concluded with a call for agreement and clarity across all interested sectors on the meanings of "non-commercial "and "commercial" usage, pursuant to ensuring that the academic community can be served while at the same time the cultural-heritage sector picture libraries can continue to make ends meet.

In 2003, Cedergren[103] examined open-content value chains, suggesting that the presence of commercial exploitation of value might be neutral in effect on motivation of creators. Further experience may or may not confirm this, though many who cite his First Monday article find the proposition appealing. Intelligent Television[104] has conducted detailed investigations in the economics of open content and organised the Economics of Open Content Symposium[105] in January 2006, exploring these ideas from a number of points of view. The symposium is available in the form of webcasts from WGBH Forum Network, a Boston public-broadcasting service. (Note that a number of open-content initiatives have benefited from significant funding support from the William and Flora Hewlett Foundation, including this symposium and the Open Content Alliance.) The Creative Archive[106] experiment, and various open-content and open-courseware initiatives suggest a collegiate, parity-based approach that provides opportunities for partnership among academic and other cultural- and scientific-heritage sector organisations, sometimes involving commercial-sector organisations as well. The vision, studies and steps toward realising the vision set out in the rest of this book depend on such an approach.

References

1. British Library. Treasures in full: High-quality digital editions, free to your desktop.
   http://www.bl.uk/treasures/treasuresinfull.html
   Note: this includes Shakespeare's plays, Magna Carta, Chaucer's *Canterbury Tales* and Gutenberg's Bible among others, some in more than one edition.

2. British Pathé Limited
   http://www.britishpathe.com/

3. British Library. Newspapers Digitisation Project: *British Newspapers 1800-1900*.
   http://www.bl.uk/collections/britishnewspapers1800to1900.html

4. University of Reading. The Farmers Weekly in Retrospect. news press release 18 May 2004
   http://www.extra.rdg.ac.uk/news/details.asp?ID=367

5. Museum of English Rural Life. Online Exhibitions: Glass Negatives.
   http://www.ruralhistory.org/online_exhibitions/glass_neg/index.html

6. Adobe. Photoshop Elements [for Macintosh]
   http://www.adobe.com/uk/products/photoshopelmac/

7. Adobe. Photoshop Elements [for Windows]
   http://www.adobe.com/uk/products/photoshopelwin/

8. GIMP (GNU Image Manipulation Program)
   http://www.gimp.org

9. BBC. *Your news, your pictures*
   http://news.bbc.co.uk/1/hi/talking_point/2780295.stm

10. Acres of innovation – so what can video do for you? *Online Press Gazette*,
    Thursday 23 November 2006
    http://www.pressgazette.co.uk/article/231106/acres_of_innovation_video

11. BBC-VJ
    http://www.bbc.co.uk/radio1/onemusic/vjing/ and VJ Central at http://www.
    vjcentral.com/

12. Flickr
    http://www.flickr.com/

13. deviantART: where ART meets application!
    http://www.deviantart.com/

14. MySpace
    http://www.myspace.com/

15. Enquiring Minds – digital tools.
    http://www.enquiringminds.org.uk/resources/digital_tools/

16. Kemp, Dave. *Artistic Statement* page on *Image Matter* web site.
    http://davekemp.ca/imagematter/xhtml/statement.htm

17. Dalwood, Alison. *Alison Dalwood – Text*. Berlin, March 2006.
    http://www.alisondalwood.co.uk/index_2.htm

18. Field of Vision
    http://www.field-of-vision.net/

19. Wright, Michael. September 2005. *Faculty for the Creative and Cultural Industries:
    research. events. CREAC research group. centre for research in electronic art and
    communication. Exhibition 6 January 2005*
    http://www.herts.ac.uk/artdes1/research/creac/event060105.html

20. Media Grid
    http://mediagrid.org/

21. *Media Grid Takes a Step Forward*. Grid Today.
    http://www.gridtoday.com/grid/760546.html
    This feature article provides news of a collaboration with Sun Microsystems.

22. Peekaboom, © Carnegie-Mellon University
    http://www.peekaboom.org/

23. Electronic Beowulf
    http://www.uky.edu/~kiernan/eBeowulf/guide.htm

24. Prescott, Andrew. 'Constructing Electronic Beowulf', in *Towards the Digital Library: The British Library's Initiatives for Access Programme*, edited by Leona Carpenter, Simon Shaw and Andrew Prescott (British Library, 1998)

25. Harley, Diane, et al. *Use and Users of Digital Resources: A Focus on Undergraduate Education in the Humanities.* Center for Studies in Higher Education, UC Berkeley (April 2006).

26. Bioscience ImageBank
http://www.bioscience.heacademy.ac.uk/imagebank/

27. Higher Education Academy Centre for Bioscience ImageBank
http://www.bioscience.heacademy.ac.uk/imagebank/

28. British Academy. *Copyright and research in the humanities and social sciences.* September 2006.
http://www.britac.ac.uk/reports/copyright/index.html

29. Creative Commons
http://creativecommons.org/

30. Images – Creative Commons
http://creativecommons.org/image/

31. Creative Commons UK
http://www.creativecommons.org.uk/

32. Youngs, Karla, and Grant Young. *Submission to the Gowers Review from the Technical Advisory Service for Images (TASI)* Institute for Learning and Research Technology, University of Bristol. 19 April 2006.
http://www.hm-treasury.gov.uk/media/51D/08/technical_advisory_service_for_images_173_108kb.pdf

33. Gowers Review of Intellectual Property. HM Treasury – Independent reviews.
http://www.hm-treasury.gov.uk/independent_reviews/gowers_review_intellectual_property/gowersreview_index.cfm

34. Naomi Korn: Copyright Consultancy
http://www.naomikorn.com/

35. Korn, Naomi. *Guide to Intellectual Property Rights and Other Legal Issues*, Version 1.0, © 2005 Minerva Project, p14-15.
http://www.minervaeurope.org/publications/guideipr1_0.pdf

36. TASI: Advice – File Formats and Compression
http://www.tasi.ac.uk/advice/creating/fileformat.html

37. TASI: Advice – Vector and Animated Graphics
http://www.tasi.ac.uk/advice/vector/vector.html

38. IMKA Project
(MetaSEEk was subsumed into this Intelligent Multimedia Knowledge Application project.)
http://www.ee.columbia.edu/~ana/imka/

39. CLEF Cross Language Image Retrieval Track (imageCLEF): Text and/or Content-Based Cross Language Image Retrieval and Annotation
http://ir.shef.ac.uk/imageclef/

40. Ward, A., Graham, M., Riley, J., Eliot, N., Eakins, J., Sheen, N. and Pringle, C. 'Collage and content-based image retrieval: Collaboration for enhanced services for the London Guildhall Library', *Museums and the Web 2001* (2001).
http://www.archimuse.com/mw2001/papers/ward/ward.html

41. Ward, A. A., Graham, M. E., Riley, K. J. and Sheen, N. 'Enhancing a historical digital art collection: Evaluation of content-based image retrieval on collage', *Digital Art History A Subject in Transition* (2005) (Eds. A. Bentkowska-Kafel, T. Cashen and H. Gardiner), Intellect Books, pp.101-112.

42. Eakins, J., Graham, M. *Content-based Image Retrieval*. JISC Technology Applications Programme Report 39, 1999.
http://www.jisc.ac.uk/uploaded_documents/jtap-039.doc

43. Virage
http://www.virage.com/home/index.en.html

44. Addis, M., Lewis, P., Martinez, K. 'ARTISTE image retrieval system puts European galleries in the picture', Cultivate Interactive, issue 7, 11 July 2002
http://www.cultivate-int.org/issue7/artiste/

45. ARTISTE Project. artiste: an integrated art analysis and navigation environment
http://www.it-innovation.soton.ac.uk/artiste/

46. Accessing and researching great art online. IST Results.
http://istresults.cordis.europa.eu/index.cfm/section/news/tpl/article/
BrowsingType/Features/ID/68144

47. Bird, C.L., Elliott, P.J., and Hayward, P.M. 'Content-Based Retrieval for European Image Libraries'. Challenge of Image Retrieval, Newcastle upon Tyne, UK. 25-26 February 1999

48. Sculpteur (Semantic and content-based multimedia exploitation for European benefit)
http://www.sculpteurweb.org/

49. University of Southampton IT Innovation Centre
http://www.it-innovation.soton.ac.uk/

50. imgSeek
http://www.imgseek.net/

51. imgSEEK [sic] tests
http://www.sculpteur.ecs.soton.ac.uk/cbr/imgSEEK.html

52. GNU General Public License. GNU project. Free Software Foundation (FSF).
http://www.gnu.org/copyleft/gpl.html

53. WebSEEk: A Content-Based Image and Video Search and Catalog Tool for the Web. Columbia University.
http://persia.ee.columbia.edu:8008/

54. QBIC(TM) – IBM's Query By Image Content
http://wwwqbic.almaden.ibm.com/

55. AHDS Visual Arts
http://ahds.ac.uk/visualarts/

56. IMAGINE – Images, Museums and Galleries in the North East.
http://www.imagine.org.uk/

57. 'Content-based image retrieval', Wikipedia
http://en.wikipedia.org/wiki/CBIR

58. Austin, I. 'Pictures, with Map and Pushpin Included.' New York Times, Nov 2, 2006.
(Available via nytimes.com; requires registration and may require payment of fee for access.)

59. Photoshare Info. The INFO Project – Capturing global efforts to improve public health and development.
http://www.photoshare.org/

60. del.icio.us – social bookmarking
http://del.icio.us/

61. ESP Game, © Carnegie-Mellon University
http://www.espgame.org/

62. Phetch, © Carnegie-Mellon University
http://www.peekaboom.org/phetch/

63. Sandhana, Lakshmi. This is a computer on your brain. *Wired News* (07/12/06).
http://www.wired.com/news/technology/medtech/0,71364-0.html?tw=wn_technology_2

64. TASI. Resources. Controlling your language – Links to Metadata Vocabularies
http://www.tasi.ac.uk/resources/vocabs.html

65. BUBL Link Catalogue of Internet Resources. *BUBL Link: Internet resources by type. Image collections.*
http://bubl.ac.uk/link/types/images.htm

66. The European Library (TEL)
http://www.theeuropeanlibrary.org/portal/index.html

67. British Association of Picture Libraries and Agencies (BAPLA)
http://www.bapla.org

68. The Visual and Sound Materials (VSM) portal scoping study and demonstrator project
http://www.jisc.ac.uk/whatwedo/programmes/programme_portals/project_vsmportal.aspx

69. Arts and Humanities Data Service (AHDS)
http://ahds.ac.uk/

70. MILE – Metadata Image Library Exploitation
http://europa.eu.int/information_society/activities/econtentplus/projects/cult/mile/index_en.htm

71. eContent*plus* Programme
http://europa.eu.int/information_society/activities/econtentplus/index_en.htm

72. pic4press
http://www.pass4press.com/cgi-bin/wms.pl/417

73. National Occupational Standards (NOS) in Photo Imaging and Photo Processing. Skillset, The Sector Skills Council for the Audio Visual Industries.
http://www.skillset.org/standards/developments/article_1925_1.asp

74. PLANETS
http://www.planets-project.eu/

75. ARKive – Images of life on Earth
http://www.arkive.org/

76. Picture Australia
http://www.pictureaustralia.org/

77. Picture Australia – Flickr
http://www.pictureaustralia.org/Flickr.html

78. ILRT – Institute for Learning and Research Technology
http://www.ilrt.bristol.ac.uk/

79. The ARKive-ERA (ARKive Educational Repurposing of Assets) Project
http://www.ilrt.bris.ac.uk/projects/project?search=ARKive-ERA

80. ILRT Imaging
http://www.ilrt.bris.ac.uk/projects/imaging

81. National Library of Australia
http://www.nla.gov.au/

82. Pearce, J. 'User Collaboration in Websites'. Staff Papers. National Library of Australia online. This paper was presented at *Framing the Future*, ARLIS/ANZ Conference, 21-23 September 2006.
http://www.nla.gov.au/nla/staffpaper/2006/jpearce1.html

83. Hooton, F. 'Democratising History: Evaluating PictureAustralia's flickr [sic] Pilot Project'. *Gateways*, Number 84, December 2006, National Library of Australia.
http://www.nla.gov.au/pub/gateways/issues/84/story13.html

84. Dempsey, L. 'National Library of Australia 2.0'. Lorcan Dempsey's weblog, 8 October 2006
http://orweblog.oclc.org/archives/001169.html

85. SCRAN
http://www.scran.ac.uk/

86. Corbis: photography, rights, assignment, motion.
http://pro.corbis.com/

87. Getty Images: Stock Photography, Royalty-Free Images, Film Footage and More.
http://creative.gettyimages.com/

88. eChase (electronic Cultural Heritage made Accessible for Sustainable Exploitation)
http://www.echase.org/

89. Eduserv Athens
http://www.athensams.net/

90. Open Content. OSS Wiki
http://wiki.oss-watch.ac.uk/OpenContent

91. Open Content Alliance
http://www.opencontentalliance.org/

92. The UK Access Management Federation For Education and Research
http://www.ukfederation.org.uk/

93. Shibboleth. Internet2
http://shibboleth.internet2.edu/

94. BECTA (British Educational Communication and Technology Agency
http://www.becta.org.uk

95. JANET UK
http://www.ja.net/about/index.html

96. ARTstor
http://www.artstor.org/info/

97. Federation Gateways. Eduserv Athens.
http://www.athensams.net/federations/federation_gateways.html/

98. SCAMP (Scottish Collections Access Management Portal)
http://scone.strath.ac.uk/scamp/

99. Teets, M., Murray, P. 'Metasearch Authentication and Access Management'.
D-Lib Magazine Volume 12 Number 6, June 2006.
http://www.dlib.org/dlib/june06/teets/06teets.html

100. JORUM
http://www.jorum.ac.uk/

101. Museums Copyright Group
http://www.museumscopyright.org.uk/

102. Connecting Commerce and Culture: Getting the Right Balance
http://www.digitalconsultancy.net/mcg2007/

103. Cedergren, M. 'Open Content and Value Creation' First Monday, volume 8,
number 8 (August 2003)
http://www.firstmonday.org/issues/issue8_8/cedergren/index.html

104. Intelligent Television
http://www.intelligenttelevision.com/

105. The Economics of Open Content Symposium. WGBH Forum Network. Free
online Lectures.
(The symposium held 23-24 January 2006, at MIT [Massachusetts Institute of
Technology] was organised by Intelligent Television with the support of the
Hewlett Foundation and MIT Open Courseware.)
http://forum.wgbh.org/wgbh/forum.php?lecture_id=0197

106. Creative Archive
http://creativearchive.bbc.co.uk/

Further reading

ALIPR™. Automatic Linguistic Indexing of Pictures – Real Time
'The ALIPR (pronounced a-lip-er), launched officially on November 1, 2006, is a
machine-assisted image tagging and searching service being developed at Penn
State by Professors Jia Li and James Z. Wang.'
http://www.alipr.com/

BioMed Image Archive
http://www.brisbio.ac.uk/index.html

Dekhtyar, A., Iacob, E., Jaromczyk, J., Kiernan, K., Moore, N. and Porter,
D. 'Building Image-based Electronic Editions using the Edition Production
Technology' TCDL Bulletin, Volume 2, Issue 1, Current 2005.
http://www.ieee-tcdl.org/Bulletin/v2n1/dekhtyar/dekhtyar.html

Domestic Interiors Database. Centre for the Study of the Domestic Interior.
Royal College of Art, Victoria and Albert Museum, and Bedford Centre, Royal
Holloway, University of London.
'It is conceived primarily as a scholarly research tool that includes textual and
visual sources and points the researcher towards analytical issues associated
with representing the interior. It also helps identify useful source materials for
specific research projects.'
http://www.rca.ac.uk/csdi/didb/

iBase Media Services
'… specialists in complete solutions for image management software and the
storage, organisation and retrieval of media files of all types. … image and
digital asset management solutions which are suitable for a broad range of
sectors, including heritage, culture, academic, corporate and scientific.'
http://www.ibase.com/home

photobucket: Video and Image Sharing
http://photobucket.com/

Shugrina, M., Betke, M., Colomosse, J.P. 'Empathic Painting: Interactive
stylization using observed emotional state.' *In Proceedings 4th Intl. Symposium on
Non-photorealistic Rendering and Animation (NPAR 2006), pages 87-96, June (2006).*
ACM Press.
An abstract, examples and link to downloadable document in PDF format from:
http://www.cs.bath.ac.uk/~vision/empaint/

Stanza. *Public Domain by stanza....2005. An artwork using CCTV and collected
images from Nottingham.*
http://www.stanza.co.uk/publicdomain/information.html

VisitorsStudio. About VisitorsStudio.
'Through simple and accessible facilities, the VisitorsStudio web-based interface
allows users to upload, manipulate and collage their own audio-visual files with
others', to remix existing media.'
http://www.visitorsstudio.org/about_vs.html

Chapter 3

the Digital Picture: A Future for Digital Images in UK Arts Education

Mike Pringle
Director, AHDS Visual Arts

Brandstrup's work in the White Christmas show at The Place, 29th November 2005 as part of an AHRC fellowship ...nn Robinson.

the Digital Picture

http://thedigitalpicture.ac.uk/home.html

The rapid rise of digital technology has led many visual arts educators to express concern over the demise of the traditional institutional slide library built to meet pedagogical needs and course requirements. Although a range of online image collections – both free and subscription based – is available to higher and further education institutions, no single collection is comprehensive enough to meet the diverse needs of all users, nor is it viable for institutions to subscribe to all the collections. Further, such collections often include an eclectic mix that does not meet specific educational and academic requirements.

the Digital Picture initiative reported here has identified a number of core problems for arts education, including the lack of appropriate images, copyright restrictions, resource discovery and lack of common technical standards and best-practice guidance. In consultation with the arts education community, it explored solutions to these problems. The community consultation identified a diversity of views and needs which make clear that there is no single solution. However, a virtual national repository for images that would allow institutions to house their own digital image collections, allow teachers and academics to deposit images, and allow institutions to share images, would be a first stepping stone. Such a repository requires a sustainable model to provide open access and should comply with JISC Information Environment standards, ensuring interoperability and ease of access.

Caren Milloy
JISC Collections Manager

Introduction

This chapter presents the results that emerged from *the* Digital Picture project. Proposed and run by AHDS Visual Arts (the visual arts centre for the Arts and Humanities Data Service), the project was designed to establish an overview of issues, and potential solutions, relating to the use and impact of digital images within visual arts higher education institutes and associated organisations. The core of the project was a national consultation with communities involved in or concerned with the use of digital images in arts education and research.

Logo from *the* Digital Picture project
© AHDS, *The* Digital Picture.

the Digital Picture grew directly from a desire within arts education communities to explore changes associated with the rise of digital images and their supporting technologies within arts education. By giving a voice to everyone in our art colleges and university departments, in all parts of the UK and at every level, the project was created to identify clear ways for the community, as a whole, to erase the problems with, and embrace the strengths of, images in the digital age.

the Digital Picture's *raison d'être* can be summarised as follows:

the Digital Picture has been established to explore issues relating to the effects of the digital revolution on our use of images. It will identify problems and develop practical solutions; liaise with stakeholders and interested parties; and offer guidance to teaching, learning and research communities.

Initiated in 2004, the project was proposed in a paper entitled The National Digital Image Initiative[1]. The paper emerged as a result of AHDS Visual Arts' close connections with the arts education community and a corresponding awareness of a number of common fears and worries across that community, relating to the ubiquitous rise of digital technologies.

One of the fundamental drivers of *the* Digital Picture project was to give people within the arts education community an opportunity to voice their thoughts, concerns and ideas relating to the use and impact of digital images in their world. It can often appear that important decisions about information and communication technology (ICT) in education, whether they be about funding or strategic development, are based solely on synthesised versions of events, rather than directly relating to the very people who will be affected. Consequently, the most important aspect of this chapter is the actual results – what the community says. Nonetheless, the next section does offer a brief discussion of what the consultation raised, though it should be taken in the context of AHDS Visual Arts' view of the project. For a more complete picture, the full results of the consultation are available on *the* Digital Picture website[2].

Discussion

It is clear, from the results of *the* Digital Picture, that there are serious concerns within the arts education community relating to the impact of digital technologies on arts education and, in some ways, on the arts in general. However, the real fears relating to digital images are as much to do with educational processes and pedagogical values as with the quality of JPGs or the latest imaging software.

Much of the fear lies in the speed of change, and in concerns that there is a lack of forethought and consideration for any negative impact that such change brings. Furthermore, the new technology seems to threaten livelihoods and the essential qualities of 'human' skills, with an apparent shift away from traditional expertise and resources towards increased 'virtual learning' and reliance on online materials with all its attendant problems: difficulties finding the right images for study; problems of reliable provenance and image quality; problems of ownership and licensing costs; and problems relating to educational agendas being led by technological advances. And, for tutors and students alike, there is a perceived lack of support and investment for the new technologies across the sector. In particular, there are fears that, although a balance of old and new is to be desired, financial and strategic imperatives mean that this is unlikely to happen. Institutes will not, the community believes, maintain 'out-of-date' equipment and practices because of issues with cost, space, expertise and, increasingly, health and safety.

Despite such concerns, the consultation has clearly demonstrated that, overall, the community is keen to embrace the new technology, but in a measured and informed way, and in a manner that would complement, rather than replace, traditional art teaching and practice.

The Core problem

The findings of the Digital Picture confirm that arts education's most pressing problem (relating to digital images) is generally perceived as how lecturers, students, librarians et al will be able to access the images they need in light of the potential demise of the traditional slide library. By referring to the observations made by Jenny Godfrey, in her keynote speech at the ARLIS Slide Study Day in March 2004[3], the core problem can be broken down into a number of specific issues that the community feels need to be addressed:

- There is a serious lack of appropriate images (e.g. subject specific) in the digital domain
- Legal, IPR and copyright restrictions are stifling the ability to create/use digital images
- There is no usable, helpful structure for finding and obtaining images
- There is no structure for facilitating or managing 'loans' of digital images
- Formats and pixel quality are not necessarily appropriate for use
- It is difficult to share/pool digital image resources
- There is a lack of use of common standards (or of standards at all)
- Appropriate safeguards and provenance are not available
- There is a lack of resource and support for the use of digital images

Moving towards a solution

'The best option must surely be a global, subscription-based image library.'

The view expressed in this statement, taken from a questionnaire response, came up a number of times during the Digital Picture seminars. However, according to the total results of the project's survey, nearly half the community disagrees with such a proposal. 72% of respondents feel that they should have the training, time and tools to create digital images themselves; while 47% believe that their institution should deal with the issue, perhaps via an intranet, institutional repository, Virtual Learning Environment or through the library. A compromise view that met with widespread support was that of a (subject-based) one-stop shop, augmented by local facilities:

'A central resource for core images from Art and Design History, freely available, plus more specialised images made in the institution would be the ideal.'

However, although many people believe that the solution (to the provision of digital images) should involve some sort of easily accessible online facility, there is a huge range of differing opinions as to how this could be achieved. Indeed, some are sceptical that it can happen at all, because of the depth and *human* complexity of the issues surrounding such a venture. Nonetheless, an answer must be found; the arts education community needs images, and digital is here to stay.

If a one-stop shop was to be attempted, what sort of thinking would need to go into the building of such a resource? In his stimulating review of systems development, 'The Inmates Are Running The Asylum'[4], Alan Cooper observes that 'Ironically, the thing that will likely make the least improvement in the ease of use of software-based products is new technology.... The problem is one of culture, training, and attitude of the people who make them, more than it is one of chips and programming languages.' And, if we go back to the list of issues given above, we can see why an aim to create a single, online system will not work in isolation: the construction of a website/portal/gateway will not resolve the complex human issues that lie behind the paucity of digital-image access.

Perhaps a more fluid, evolutionary approach is required. Community members may be better served by a series of diverse components and methods which, through working together with common aims, could gradually move towards a future where digital image needs will be met. After all, many of the images that are required are already available in digital form (or soon will be) and a huge proportion of them are, theoretically at least, already in the public domain or 'free' for educational use. The solution to providing the arts education community with easy access to the images it needs may be about *process* not *product*; the priority, not to build a one-stop website, but to figure out how we can share information.

But there are two fundamental obstacles to such an idea: the users and the providers.

The problem with users...

Consider the breadth of different users of digital images within an 'arts education community'. As well as the obvious, simplistic definitions, such as users from vastly different subject domains (graphics, art history etc.) or those with fundamentally different roles (students, practitioners or librarians),

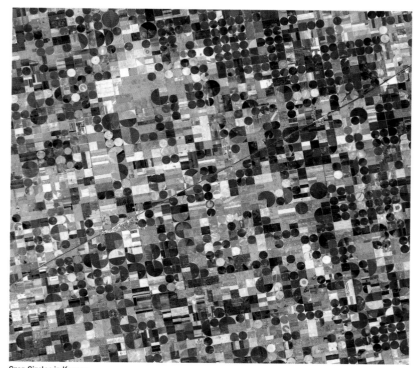

Crop Circles in Kansas
© NASA/GSFC/METI/ERSDAC/JAROS, and U.S./Japan ASTER Science Team.

there is a multitude of other ways that users can differ from one another. For example, there are users from different areas of education (non-vocational, lifelong learning, bachelor's degree, post-doctoral research etc.), or those with different learning needs (dyslexia, physical impairment, English as a second language etc.). Furthermore, we need to consider: how users of born-digital images may differ from users of digitised images; distinctions between 'digital natives' – those who have grown up in the digital environment – and 'digital immigrants' – those for whom the digital environment has been a relatively recent introduction[5]; and users of different types of images (e.g. bitmap and vector). And, of course, there is the use of the image itself: does it need to be very high quality so that the subject can be studied in detail, or will a low-resolution version do just to make a visual point?

The implications of such a wide-ranging user community are made more complex by the fact that a user can be made up of any combination of the definitions above, and can be different things at different times. Also, if we are to really understand the users, we need to accept that within each person's day-to-day life, decisions and actions are governed, not by altruistic notions of idealised image access, but by the weight of job descriptions, local politics, inter-staff relationships, trivial tasks and the simple, pragmatic need to get things done. It is also important to remember that not everyone in education wants to be an 'expert' in digital images – a ceramics tutor may want to present an illustrated lecture, making use of the facilities that are available, but he/she does not necessarily want to have to understand the intricacies of capture, cataloguing, manipulation, storage and dissemination of digital images. Add to all this the fact that the combined power of the internet, intranet, VLE and/or institutional repository presents a mind-boggling, murky multitude of 'solutions' to finding images, and the net result is that most digital image users will respond to image provision in the simplest and most appropriate way for them at the time. Usually this means Google; it won't necessarily give the ideal answer, but it will give *an* answer and, for many users in many cases, that will do.

The problem with providers...

The depth, variety and diversity of available image-focused websites raise a simple problem: how are users expected to know which site will provide the image they need? It is patently unreasonable to expect everyone who wants an image, for whatever reason, to have to visit, subscribe to and search each of these sites in turn until he/she happens to stumble on what he/she wants. The opacity of just what is available is compounded by: the different types of collections (e.g. JISC/AHRC funded, national institutions, HE providers, private); the apparent need for owners to 'brand' their own collections; multiple, different authentication procedures; frequent lack of provenance; the range of costing models; poor or vastly differing search/ navigation mechanisms; inconsistent metadata standards, when applied at all; protection of ownership rights; and the blurring of just what can be used, by whom and for what purpose.

Essentially, image providers, be they on the internet or via a local system, each offer part of the solution to providing *all* the images needed by the arts education community; a partial solution often more influenced, quite understandably, by the immovable drivers behind the scenes (e.g. funding bodies, limited collections, marketing needs, management directives or software developers), rather than the fluid and infinitely variable needs of an entire community.

Perhaps none of this would matter, if each different user could find a provider perfectly suited to him/her, giving access to all the images he/she might need in the appropriate manner and at the right time. However, even a solution like this would be far from ideal, at a broader level. Ironically, despite the differing perspectives of users across the arts education community, there is a huge overlap in the images that they need. Having different providers for different users would, and indeed does, lead to massive duplication of effort, a confusion of different image versions and a corresponding waste of financial and human resources.

Nonetheless, most people would now agree that, if a solution is to be found, it will have to be led by the needs of the users, no matter how complex such a resulting 'system' may seem. This view is already strongly recognised across the education sector, both within JISC and on a broader scale. For example, when considering repositories, the JISC-funded Digital Repositories Review states that 'it is vital that repositories *meet the needs of users*; there is a need to explore *user requirements* and prioritise them in the development of repositories; the process needs to engage the *user community* in a real way.'[6] And, on a bigger scale, the House of Commons' Education and Skills Committee report following the low uptake of the £50m UK e-University noted that it 'failed largely because it took a supply-driven rather than *demand-led* approach'[7].

In short, if we want to solve the community's digital image needs, we must first think about *what* those needs are before trying to prescribe *how* they might be met.

Yet the users' requirements, as listed above, seem clear. But still no model has been implemented for providing access to *all* the images that the arts education community needs. And, whilst user terminology is everywhere – all new online projects seem to discuss 'user needs', 'user-led development' or 'user-driven requirements' – we still see web-based resources failing to achieve the kind of uptake that might be hoped for. Only 37% of respondents to *the* Digital Picture questionnaire felt that the internet was the best place to find images, and a mere 17% believed that existing digital image resources were sufficient for research purposes. Despite the determined efforts of providers of online resources, there often seems to be a gaping chasm between what they produce and the needs of the user community.

One major reason for this is the fact that very few people are working together towards a solution; as mentioned before, most providers are governed by their own, individual drivers rather than the broader needs of the community. They are trying to meet known user needs, but only for their own target users, or in line with constraints of funding, politics, branding or available images. This is indicative of an underlying, much broader issue in education culture – essentially, that everyone who should be part of the solution is in competition with everyone else. For a solution to emerge, the culture itself needs to change. This publication is, hopefully, evidence of such change beginning to establish itself.

What the community says

Because the intention of *the* Digital Picture was to elicit a view that would be representative of an entire community, and in order that all members of that community could feel that they had an opportunity to contribute, the project held a broad, open consultation rather than, for example, questioning a small representative subsection of the arts education community. To facilitate this approach, a questionnaire was devised that enabled respondents to answer simple questions on a range of digital image subjects that were considered to be important.

This section presents the results of the consultation.

Respondent data

Respondent breakdown was as follows: 502 people completed questionnaires and 257 signed up for workshops/seminars. The website received 128,743 hits (5,814 visitor sessions) and 458 people signed up to *the* Digital Picture email list. Data regarding the role of the respondent, the educational level with which he/she was involved, and age were also collected.

Consultation results

Colour exercise-ideas sheet, 1966
© VADS Basic Design Collection.

At the outset of the project, potential issues were divided into ten broad areas and, for each of these areas, a number of responses were elicited. The following subsections (a. to k.) present a summary discussion of the results as well as a few sample responses, derived from both the questionnaire and workshop/ online debates.

a. Increase in digital images

Question
Digital images are on the increase in arts education. What overall impact does this increase have on you?

Summary

86% of respondents feel that the increase of digital images in arts education has had an impact on them. For an extremely heartening 74% this impact materialises as an improvement in the learning and teaching environment, with 66% believing that the rise in digital images helps them to be more computer literate. However, the advantages come with provisos. Only 29% of respondents are unconcerned at the corresponding loss of traditional products, skills or knowledge. It is clear, from seminar debates, that much of the fear lies in the speed with which change is occurring, and the lack of forethought and consideration for any negative impact. Also, the new technology seems to threaten livelihoods and the essential qualities of 'human' skills, with an apparent shift away from traditional expertise and resources towards increased 'virtual learning' and online materials.

Selected quotes from respondents

'I have found my increasing confidence and experience in using new technologies creatively and as an educational tool both invigorating and illuminating!'

'Can result in a loss of understanding of the physical nature of things. Digital images need to be used in conjunction with an understanding of the artefacts themselves.'

'The downside is that it is so much easier for the students to produce a large quantity of sub-standard images.'

'Digital imagery could make a much more significant impact in the learning environment if we had sufficient hardware and software resources.'

b. Fit for the purpose

Question

Digital images can be used in a number of ways, but are they better at some things than they are at others?

Summary

Overall, the community accepts that digital images are of a sufficient quality for use in their professions: 87% feel that they are excellent for talks and lectures; 74% consider them suitable for uses beyond web or intranet pages; 69% have no doubts about their usefulness for creating new artwork; andonly 22% are concerned about their quality for close examination or printing purposes. Nonetheless, heated discussions have been had about just what 'fit for purpose' means: to an art history lecturer, high resolution may be essential to make a particular point, whereas, for an FE student illustrating an essay, the subject matter may be more important than the quality of the image itself. The broad needs of such a diverse community create something of a tension when trying to identify the desirable qualities of digital images, and this in turn can impact on the way that art is taught.

Selected quotes from respondents

'A good-quality image is an excellent teaching tool.'

'Quality is a significant issue for art historians – but the tools are improving, and a more widespread understanding of acceptable digitisation standards is (slowly) developing.'

'Unfortunately, too many people and establishments view them as a cheap and faster option for working, with no consideration for the broader educational picture.'

c. Effect on traditional education

Question

What effect do digital images have on more traditional aspects of art education?

Summary

76% of respondents are adamant that traditional media and approaches should not be lost as a result of digital images, with less than half (44%) convinced that digital on-screen activity is not having an adverse effect on face-to-face contact. 37% believe that increased access to digital images is an improvement on the limitations of gallery visits but, as some of the quotes below illustrate, most feel that, ideally, students should have both. Despite these concerns, 71% feel that arts education is improved by digital images. Seminar debates on this topic revealed many other issues, relating to but not covered by the questionnaire. In particular, there were fears that, although a balance of old and new was to be desired, financial and strategic imperatives meant that this was unlikely to happen. Institutes are unlikely to maintain 'out-of-date' equipment and practices because of issues with cost, space, expertise and, increasingly, health and safety.

Selected quotes from respondents

'A balance must be struck between traditional and digital methods as both have a major role to play.'

'Poor teachers will always use a/v aids as a substitute for face-to-face interaction.'

'Whilst there is no substitute for examining an original artwork, increasing access to digital copies can only help our understanding of the topic. Imagine how "in the dark" most people were in the days before photography and the wider dissemination of artworks.'

d. Finding digital images

Question
If you wanted a particular image in digital format, what would be the ideal way to obtain it?

Summary
Finding the right digital images for use in education is a problem, particularly given quality and ownership issues, and only 37% of respondents feel that the internet currently offers the best solution to this problem. 72% feel that they should have the training, time and tools to create digital images themselves; 57% would like some sort of one-stop shop on the internet; while 47% feel that their institution should deal with the issue. However, the community recognises that these issues are complex: most understand that it is unrealistic to expect everyone to have expertise in digitisation; and, more significantly, there is widespread concern that no single person, institute or organisation can possibly provide all the images that all students/staff will require.

Selected quotes from respondents
'Hundreds of "self-scans" populating the web is very dangerous in so many ways.'

'Most academic staff would not have the facilities or expertise to create digital images of a good enough quality. This work is best left to experts in the field.'

'Ideally a core collection of images should be available from online resources accessible via a one-stop shop, but this should be supplemented by an archive produced in-house, tailor-made for the courses taught in each institution.'

'I can't imagine that a one-stop shop is a realistic aspiration.'

e. Technological resources

Question
The successful use of digital images depends on technology. What issues does this raise?

Summary

Just over half of respondents (55%) are confident that technological benefits will outweigh the related problems – the rest are not so convinced, particularly when it comes to the financial burden of technology, with only 26% believing that costs are reasonable. In many cases, also relating to costs, it appears that the arts education community is frustrated at the levels of available technological resources: only 34% feel that their institute is fully up to date, and only 40% have the tools that they require. Nonetheless, the technology does seem to have turned a corner where most people now accept it as part of their normal working day rather than as something new; the main issues, as with so many things, are to do with money, priorities and alternative agendas.

Selected quotes from respondents

'The amazing rate at which technology improves is quite scary. It's a balancing game to wait for something to come down to the right price whilst also keeping up with new technology.'

'Funding has always been a problem!'

'My institution seems prepared to pay for new technology but not for the extra staff time to set up and run the project.'

f. Usefulness

Question
Are there particular aspects of digital images that improve or reduce their usefulness?

Summary

Issues relating to the usefulness of digital images are of great concern to the arts education community: 91% think that finding images should be straightforward (unsurprisingly), and in seminar discussions it was clear that many do not believe this to be the case currently; 78% recognise the importance of an image's provenance; 82% place great importance on the inherent qualities of the image itself; and 62% believe that it is imperative that images come with associated information. These factors are fundamental

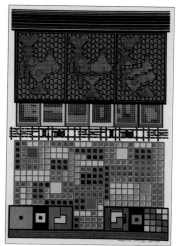

Protocol-sentences from Universal Electronic vacuum, Eduardo Paolozzi

to pedagogical practice and the community fears that the abundance of 'free' images now available to students (and lecturers), and the increased emphasis on unrestricted use of the internet, are setting misguided and sometimes dangerous precedents for arts education.

Selected Quotes from Respondents
'Reliability in terms of academic accreditation and referencing is vital.'

'Copyright is a major issue for libraries. Students need reliable and accurate metadata for referencing and citing sources.'

'Metadata is nice but not essential. If one is talking about composition or subject matter the extra information is not required.'

'Lack of metadata is what stops you from finding images.'

'Image quality is sometimes important, sometimes not.'

'Colour, contrast and clarity are, of course, important for any image. Frankly, anyone who thinks otherwise has peculiar ambitions, or is a fool.'

'The new accessibility legislation and good practice for websites require some effort to update existing sites, but the effort is worth it; while new sites can be designed with accessibility in mind from the start.'

g. Ownership

Question
Digital images can be shared and re-used very easily. Should we worry about ownership?

Summary
Copyright and IPR associated with digital images are extremely difficult areas for the arts education community. Illustrating the contradiction of a community made up of both creators and users of images, 68% acknowledge the need to protect the financial rights of image creators, whilst 75% believe the use of images should be free within education. Perhaps surprisingly, nearly half of respondents (48%) do not seem to appreciate the legal issues of downloading images from the internet. Most, it would seem, would rather have someone else sort out the problems: 79% believe their institution should take care of legal issues. Copyright will continue to be a major crippling factor in the advance of digital image use within arts education, partly because of the dilemma of creators vs. users, but more fundamentally because of a much wider 'lack of control', or 'freedom', depending on your viewpoint, with the way images can be created and shared via information communication technologies.

Selected quotes from respondents

'Intellectual property rights should never be infringed. Particularly in an educational environment where the ownership of ideas and images is a central issue.'

'People think that if it's on the web it's fair game. How it got on the web is another matter. You would not steal a book from a bookshop, so you should not steal an image from the web.'

'Educational use of copyright images should be free!'

'I think copyright issues are very important and we should teach students to respect copyright.'

'Unfair to expect individuals to be experts on IPR, so institutions should have clear policy on image use.'

h. Support in using digital images

Question
What considerations need to be made to help you get the most out of digital images in art education?

Summary
Support for the arts education community, in using digital images, has a way to go before the community feels that it is satisfactory, with 71% believing that more money needs to be spent. Only half of respondents (50%) feel

that they can already get help when needed, and a mere 23% understand their own institute's procedures for matters relating to digital images. However, 37% feel that they can get the training they need, compared with only 30% who feel that they cannot. Part of the problem here is that the community is unsure about just what it needs training in. More importantly, there are concerns that digital matters are taking over at such a pace that many people in the arts are being forced to become experts in areas that simply should not be part of their job.

Ad for AHDS Visual Arts
© AHDS.

Selected quotes from respondents

'There are more experts around such as TASI and AHDS, which are invaluable.'

'Training is always available – it's the funding for training that isn't. If you're prepared to pay for it yourself, you can easily find tailor-made training.'

'Finding images is incredibly time-consuming, which adds considerably to one's workload – this is nowhere acknowledged.'

i. Digital images in research

Question
Digital images have a role in research, but are there issues surrounding their use in this area?

Summary
Only 17% of respondents believe that existing digital image resources are sufficient for research purposes, and 76% think more digital image-related research should be carried out. The reasons why are clear: 76% think that digital images offer great opportunities for research founded on practical work; and 73% feel that they are an essential part of publishing research online.

 'More money should be made available for digital images.'

 'There is insufficient research on digital images and their production or on using digital imagery in creative learning or other learning.'

 'Yes! Much more research please!'

 'Digital imaging is making some research-active practitioners lazy and complacent, leading to a weak research base in the creative arts lacking in depth, substance, purpose and meaning.'

j. How important?

Question
Of the nine subjects outlined in the previous questions, which are the most important for you?

Summary
The responses to this question balanced out quite evenly over the nine subject areas: no single subject stood out as being particularly more important than any other. This is to be expected and is indicative of the fact that a large variety of different respondents were included with varying perspectives and priorities. The subject given least importance was the issue of 'digital images in research', but this almost certainly reflects a lower proportion of researchers among the overall make-up of respondents.

Selected quotes from respondents
 'At different times I'm an institutional manager, an arts manager, an educationalist, a staff developer, a writer, a researcher, a curator, a presenter and a photographer – all of these questions are important!'

 'I think this research is tremendously important and would be very interested in the results and outcomes from the consultation.'

k. General comments

Beyond the questions themselves, the questionnaire, website and email list permitted respondents to add general or additional comments; for example:

'As an art student I find that digital images are very important in the learning process, research, developing, manipulating and for final outcomes it allows us to explore another medium and express our work in various ways.'

'In many cases the students are leading the way; it is their expectation that material of all kinds should be available digitally.'

'I'm pleased by your demand-driven, rather than supply-driven approach, since other initiatives don't seem to have learnt from the UKeUniversity mistakes.'

'Such a wealth at our fingertips!'

'The internet gives us the greatest ever opportunity to provide public access at many levels to our visual heritage.'

'I love the struggle of shoving paint around on a surface but also love the instant gratification of a photo. Digital even better.'

'[the computer] is a tool, a tool to be used to extend our vocabulary of the visual world.'

'Art surely lies in the intention of the maker whether it uses paint or programming.'

'It's surely a matter of finding a balance between the possibilities created by new technology whilst not throwing the baby out with the bath water.'

Conclusion

the Digital Picture project has enabled the arts education community to articulate many of its concerns, doubts and fears about the increasing dependence on digital media for access to the most essential of its resource needs. As mentioned above, the community's main issue seems to relate to how people will be able to access the images they need in light of the potential demise of the traditional slide library. Perhaps, as a result of this project, and the other work of the Images Working Group (IWG), the future may offer a path towards resolving such an issue. In a relatively short space of time facilitating processes could exist that, in the words of the IWG's vision document: allow institutions to house their own digital image collections; allow teachers and academics to deposit images created for educational purposes; allow institutions to share image collections and provide users with online access 24/7; provide the scaffolding for other public-sector image-collection owners to add their collections; allow sustainability as a national service within a secure environment; create a critical mass of images with high relevance to education; be an open-access service and therefore engender a great sense of ownership; comply with JISC Information Environment standards, ensuring interoperability and ease of access.

References

1. The National Digital Image Initiative
   http://www.thedigitalpicture.ac.uk/documents/index.html

2. Final report is available online:
   http://www.thedigitalpicture.ac.uk/documents/index.html

3. Godfrey, J., 2004, 'A digital future for slide libraries?' *Art Libraries Journal*, vol. 29, no. 1, pp. 10-22

4. Cooper, A., 1999, *The Inmates Are Running the Asylum*, SAMS (A Division of Macmillan Computer Publishing), Indiana, USA

5. Prensky, M., 2001, 'Digital Natives, Digital Immigrants', *On the Horizon*, NCB University Press, vol. 9, no. 5
   http://www.marcprensky.com/writing/default.asp

6. Anderson, S. and Heery, R., 2005, Digital Repositories Review, para. 4.1; pg 15
   http://www.jisc.ac.uk/uploaded_documents/digital-repositories-review-2005.pdf

7. House of Commons' Education & Skills Committee, 2004-2005, *'UK e-University'*: *3rd Report*, summary p. 3

Chapter 4

Bridging the Gap: Investigating Community-Led Image Collections

Jonathan Miller & Peter Robinson, Learning Technologies
Group, University of Oxford; Rupert Shepherd, Ashmolean
Museum, University of Oxford; Karla Youngs & Grant
Young, Technical Advisory Service for Images

s, traffic – Gare do Oriente, Lisbon, Portugal
ona Carpenter.

d. Trivandrum, Kerala, India
chel Bruce.

Bridging the Gap: Investigating Community-Led Image Collections

http://www.oucs.ox.ac.uk/ltg/projects/clic

There are countless images in community image collections in the UK. The potential of these collections to contribute to education and research is vast and, until now, largely untapped. The images are often held in discrete silos, often filestores on desktop machines that are either not networked at all, or networked on an *ad hoc* basis within a single department or, at best, institution. The authors of this chapter have an alternative vision, whereby such collections can be easily discovered, and their contents browsed and searched, alongside those of other collections. The challenges in achieving this vision should not be underestimated, and the authors make it clear that the road is unlikely to be either smooth or short; but it is navigable and, in the JISC Information Environment Technical Architecture and the overarching vision laid out in Chapter One, we have a guide, at least to the technical aspects. The organisational and strategic challenges are at least as great, though, and (as with all the studies reported in this book) the way to address these is as a partnership between a wide range of relevant bodies, including JISC, services such as TASI and Intute, the Higher Education Academy, Becta, and those working outside education (museums, libraries, archives, commercial image providers and so on). The advantages of leveraging community image collections make this partnership approach worthwhile. Each collection is embedded in a community, is built by and through that community's practices, and is likely to be configured for use by that community. The resulting collection is, both in its contents and in its organisation, rich in tacit knowledge about that community. This is both the promise and the challenge of sharing such collections.

Neil Jacobs
JISC Programme Manager

Introduction

Online collections of digital images have burgeoned in recent years and, at the same time, advances in affordable digital photography and home scanning have empowered teachers and researchers to create their own digital images. However, usage of image collections in teaching and learning has not flourished to the same degree, despite the funding of a number of technical initiatives to provide access to nationally hosted image collections.

The Community-Led Image Collection (CLIC) scoping study was commissioned by the JISC to review current community image collection activity and make recommendations about how national initiatives could help embed collections within the wider educational community, to provide better access to high-quality educational image material.

The study was a collaboration between the Learning Technologies Group, at the University of Oxford, and the Technical Advisory Service for Images (TASI)[1], at the University of Bristol, and undertook the following activities:

- An overview of current community image collection activity, by consultation with collection providers

- Selecting community image collections to use as case studies

- Surveying image owners and users via workshops and surveys

- An investigation of viable models for a network of image collections to promote sharing of image resources

Pistoia
© Seamus Ross.

Defining the problem

Figure 4.1 shows various sources of image material available to the academic community. Academics who want to find image material may use Google or refer to institutional or local collections. If they cannot find the material they want instantly, they give up. Barriers such as authorisation (from, for example, library membership or online subscription) prevent access by both search engines and 'unauthorised' users. Internet search engines serve the commercial sector, and are not geared towards providing high-quality educational resources, so many of the collections funded recently do not feature prominently in their search results. This leads to what we describe as the discovery gap – the educational community being unable to easily locate images that have been provided for their use.

Figure 4.1
The Discovery Gap

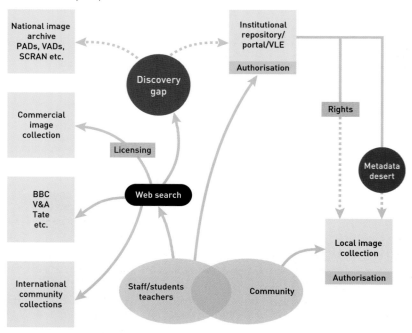

Castle Grayskull (for He-Man Marvel comic)
© Mike Pringle.

Method

Identifying existing collections

In the course of its study, CLIC compiled a list of nearly 500 UK image collections, using information provided by TASI's Image Collection Registry, the Resource Discovery Network[2] (RDN, currently being re-branded as Intute[3]) and various funding bodies. These were mainly arts and humanities collections, perhaps because the science communities have already created large community portals to meet their needs, in which images are stored as part of general research. An example of this is the EMBL (European Molecular Biology Laboratories)[4] Nucleotide Sequence Database. The majority of the collections that we found were not 'image databases'; rather, they were websites that contained significant amounts of information that put the image into context.

Proposed models

The CLIC project held a workshop at which the following models for collection provision were discussed:

- National collections of images for each subject area

- A nationally maintained online subscription service of high-quality licensed images

- A national online system or portal of catalogue information, linking to local collections

- A shared store of copyright-cleared images provided by members of the educational community

- A support network for autonomous local collections (e.g. providing technical support, directory services)

There was little support for a subscription service, and image providers were not keen to donate their images directly to a central repository. Image collection providers felt that a national service might marginalise them, particularly if the system's interface removed the user from the original collection and its surrounding material. We did find support both for a central directory of image collections and for a system to hold catalogue information.

Survey of image providers

We compiled a questionnaire and sent it to all the collections identified in the list. There were 81 responses, from which we were able to determine the following profile of a typical image collection:

- Built as a bespoke system running on a dedicated server in-house, providing open access via the web

- Contains over 1,000 images and expects to grow to contain 10,000 images within two years

- Not targeted specifically at education, though it has a policy on the educational use of images

- Provides information about items in its collection as Dublin Core metadata[5], if it provides metadata at all

- Would expect acknowledgement and attribution of the collection as the source of any material reused

- Wants to maintain copyright over the images in its collection

- Would expect payment for high-quality printing or commercial reuse of its images

- Does not watermark its images, though it states its ownership of the images held on the site

- Considers time, money and technical knowledge to be the greatest barriers to future development of the collection
- Would like technical support and marketing assistance from a centralised service

The research questions posed by the survey are given below, together with a summary of the responses.

What are the key barriers to growth, and what are the technical support needs that could be addressed centrally?

The major hurdle in collection building was lack of time (cited by 56% of the providers); next was insufficient funding (54%) and then lack of technical knowledge. The most popular request was for technical support (46%), followed by marketing (42%) and then search facilities (41%). The latter two again suggest support for a searchable directory of collections held nationally. The providers also mentioned, unsurprisingly, that lack of funding and the difficulty of raising funds after an initial digitisation project had ended were a barrier to growth.

What support is there for a federated network or service?

The survey asked image providers to consider three options: a directory of collections, a directory of catalogue information and a national collection of image material. Respondents to our survey were wary of how a centralised service would affect them, expressing the fear that it would lead to marginalisation of smaller collections. The responses to our question about a centralised service showed that:

- 84% support a central directory of image collections
- 76% support a service holding metadata from image collections
- 31% support donation of their images to a central image repository/ collection

What metadata exists locally that could be exposed to a national service (portal or directory)?

Most image providers did not have sophisticated systems to allow metadata to be harvested or exported. This meant that the exposure of collections' catalogue information for cross-searching would be difficult. The metadata standard most commonly mentioned by providers was Dublin Core, occasionally because their own internal cataloguing could be mapped to it.

Is the collection part of a community? Is there a demand for sharing material?

Nearly all collections served one or more subject-based communities. The provider of one particularly large medical collection felt it to be relevant to a number of subjects, including history and design and technology. The majority of the providers accepted donations from people with material relevant to their collection, with some actively seeking out material and others fulfilling requests from viewers. Around 62% had contributions from people outside the immediate organisation. Surprisingly few collections allowed viewers to annotate the material online.

What are the collection owners' attitudes to sharing and allowing open access for educational use?

The vast majority of collections surveyed were open-access web collections that allowed an unregistered guest to view the thumbnail image and the associated higher quality image. Broadly speaking, the majority of collections were happy for the images to be used for individual research, or by an individual for educational purposes. However, most respondents felt that sharing images more widely would result in unauthorised commercial reuse, publication without recompense and loss of copyright control. The most common concerns raised were as follows:

Common concerns about image sharing	Number of respondents
Loss of copyright control	25
Unauthorised commercial reuse	21
Lack of attribution	8
Ethical concerns	7
Unconcerned	5
Don't own copyright	5

Some providers had very few concerns, adopting the attitude that the purpose of the site was to provide greater access to the material:

A common policy was to publish images of low quality or small pixel dimensions as a deterrent against misuse. Neither textual marks on the images nor formal encrypted watermarks were popular. Only one respondent mentioned a formal, Creative Commons[6] (CC) licence for reuse being attached to their material.

Concern about misuse was tempered by widespread agreement that the material could be used for private research or by an individual for educational purposes – uses already permitted under the 'fair dealing' aspect of UK copyright law.

The CLIC Three-Tier Model

Meeting the needs of providers and users

During the study we found that the biggest barrier to sharing images among individuals, institutions and communities was lack of trust. Technical barriers can be overcome, but a technical solution in no way guarantees the success of image sharing. The problem is social, not technical. Collection providers need to be able to trust that the material they provide will only be used in ways that they find acceptable, and that their ownership and IPR will be respected.

Trust needs to be built within and between institutions, so that image-based teaching materials provided by one party will be made available for use by another, and so that all parties can rely on the veracity of information provided in image collections.

Trust is particularly important when dealing with high-risk material such as images of children or those that can be used to identify individuals. Images that are subject to copyright should be clearly distinguishable from those in the public domain and any restrictions on the use of images should be easily understood.

Henna Hand
© Balviar Notay.

In order to make low-risk material available, while at the same time restricting access to high-risk material, our study proposed the establishment of community-based image collections that are situated between existing local and national collections, creating a three-tier system:

1. Local collections of high-risk material held within trusted communities of practice

2. Open-access community repositories with devolved management of low-risk submissions from HE/FE. These communities of practice would only hold material that was rights-cleared under Creative Commons (or similar) licences. Management would be devolved to self-organising, subject-based communities of practice with minimal staff support

3. National Image Collections incorporating rights-cleared low-risk material from the community repositories, and reciprocating by providing low-risk, rights-cleared material from their own holdings

Selous Game Reserve, Tanzania
© Caren Milloy.

Figure 4.2

Proposed three-tier model for linking image collections

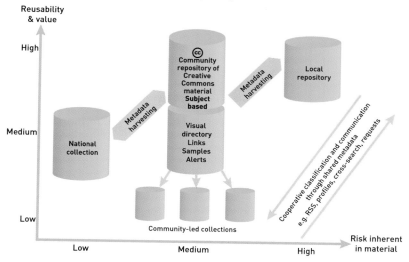

In order to function together, all three systems will require the following common attributes:

- A system for the syndication and aggregation of discovery information
- Local authentication and authorisation controls for high-risk material
- Metadata harvesting mechanisms
- Consolidation of marketing opportunities
- Community-led requests for additional material
- Cooperative classification and communication through shared metadata
- Higher-risk material to be held locally, lower-risk material to be shared
- Implementation based on open standards

Intellectual property rights

The success of the model relies on providing a subset of material central to specific subjects and, critically, material that does not need rights clearance. This material should be provided by the community, but some may need to be funded specifically for the project. This material must be 'born digital', with no prior copyright, and licensed in perpetuity. Legacy legal and IPR issues have the potential to cripple development of the model in its early stages, as has happened to a number of the digitisation and resource-creation schemes studied.

The success of the CC icons for labelling online resources and the consistent use of associated licence hypertext has allowed search engines such as Yahoo (http://search.yahoo.com/cc) and Google's Advanced search to return material licensed under agreed conditions (such as for non-commercial reuse). This approach will promote automatic discovery of shareable content by search engines.

Our investigations, and also *the* Digital Picture survey[7], revealed significant confusion over what an end user can do with material obtained from a website or repository. The US concept of 'fair use' of materials is often wrongly ascribed to the UK copyright situation. Image users need a simple way to discover material that is free for use in teaching and learning, and that carries with it a consistent and easy-to-understand set of licences.

A policy decision should be made regarding the cost-effectiveness of developing a new licence to govern the sharing and reuse of image material. Considerable work has already been done by the Creative Commons community on localising their licences for the UK legal systems and this inspired the Creative Archive[8] consortium to create UK-specific licences. Significant time and effort could be wasted on the drafting or adaptation of licences to address the perceived uniqueness of the educational field. If it is decided that existing licences are not suitable, OSS Watch (the open source software advisory service) and other relevant JISC legal working groups should be consulted early in the process to advise on alternatives. It is vital to achieve the goal of an initial set of material with absolutely clear guidelines on licensing, attribution, modification and sharing.

Creative Commons offers authors a set of licences to assign to their own material, for instance allowing material to be reused for non-commercial purposes only and with proper attribution. Creative Archive is a similar licence model, created by a consortium of public sector groups such as the BBC and the British Film Institute (BFI). Inspired by the work of Creative Commons, its licence stipulates further restrictions limiting reuse to within the UK, and allowing no endorsement and no derogatory use.

The Common Information Environment (CIE)[9] group has submitted a report on the use of Creative Commons licences by publicly funded UK organisations. The CIE study attempts to clarify the risks and potential of making publicly funded digital resources available for reuse and investigates whether Creative Commons licences might reduce digital project costs and increase the visibility and reuse of such material. The report concludes that Creative Commons is suitable for some – but not all – of the cases studied. The Museums and Libraries Association also recently agreed to pursue the Creative Commons model.

The differentiation between institutional and individual ownership of image material has profound effects on how easy it is to reach agreement on sharing materials. An individual could make an informed, instant decision on releasing material into a repository for sharing; an institution obviously cannot. From the Jorum[10] Digital Rights Management Watch 2005 report:

Lack of clarity and a common understanding regarding ownership of learning materials within institutions presents a challenge for Jorum. It may be expected that individuals will assume ownership of content that their employers would, if consulted, consider to be the property of the institution. If individuals were permitted to deposit content into Jorum, this may result in Jorum holding content with inaccurate (or disputed) rights information. It may be difficult to identify cases where the creator had incorrectly assumed ownership in ignorance. Jorum requires certainty of ownership. At present, Jorum accepts deposit only by institutions; individuals cannot deposit content directly. Thus, accuracy of rights information is the responsibility of the depositing institution; it must ensure that any staff member who is authorised to deposit has a clear understanding of ownership of rights in that content. However, this policy raises another issue. While content created in the course of employment is owned by the employer, not all learning and teaching materials used to deliver courses in UK HE/FE are owned by institutions as not all university and college teachers create their materials within the course of employment. For example, an employee who is paid an hourly rate and only for teaching hours creates the materials used for her classes outside of her employment contract and thus owns those materials.

Graffiti (close-up inset)
© Seamus Ross.

Nevertheless, the Jorum team believes that there are individuals within the community who, as rightful owners of the materials that they have created, wish to deposit those in Jorum. They could do this by assigning ownership of their materials to an institution to deposit on their behalf. However, a recent case in a Canadian University suggests that even when individuals are willing to share materials with colleagues, they wish to retain control over its integrity and use; assignment of ownership to an institution conflicts with that wish (Canadian Association of University Teachers, 2004). An alternative mechanism is available to allow individuals to deposit content in Jorum whilst retaining ownership; the owner may license her content to an institution within the JISC community and the institution may, in turn, deposit that content in Jorum (thus sub-licensing it to Jorum which, in turn, will sub-license it to Jorum users). This will allow Jorum to offer individually owned content whilst the institution bears the responsibility (and any liability arising) for it.

Whether institutions are willing to accept this liability remains to be seen.

A visual directory as marketing tool

The community image providers have already shown considerable interest in – and support for – being associated with a national visual directory and there is similar support for a sharing of collections' catalogue information. The CLIC project has already compiled a directory of 500 sites, containing an estimated 5–6 million images.

The visual directory would be hosted centrally but maintained by subject specialists such as the Higher Education Academies (HEAs)[11]. Collection owners who registered would be offered a visual directory space providing useful tools, services and structures. The following kinds of service could be offered:

- A directory of image-collection information maintained by image provider
- Simple provider/collection profile information
- The ability to host sample images from the collection in this space
- Automatic news/photofeed alerts created for every provider
- Technical support via mailing lists and bulletin boards
- Aggregation of material and links from the providers' own associations
- Marketing and access information
- Standardised contact information

The visual system should act as an encyclopedia of educational image activity. There is a precedent for this idea – Wiki Commons (http:// commons.wikimedia.org/wiki/) uses the freely available open source Wikimedia software to generate an encyclopedia of images that can be reused throughout the Wikipedia[12] project. A simple subject-based front-end and free-text search, together with searches of recent additions, would aid discovery of image material. The maintenance of each collection page should be devolved to the partner image providers.

Discovery and dissemination

The visual directory provides collection owners with a mechanism for marketing their collections and disseminating news via Really Simple Syndication (RSS) photofeeds. These feeds should be picked up by subject-based sites such as the HEAs, Intute (formerly RDN), TASI, National Grid for Learning (NGfL), British Educational Communications and Technology Agency (BECTA) and other centrally funded organisations with an interest in educational image material.

Each HEA centre and Intute hub should use an agreed icon to display links to subject-based image collections prominently on their website. Recent additions, popular search results and project news should be disseminated through RSS photofeeds.

Egypt, 2006
© Angelo Conti.

Figure 4.3
Discovery relationships between image providers and image seekers in a CLIC landscape

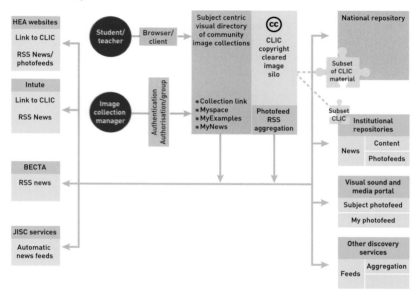

Community building

The community aspect of the CLIC three-tier model is very important. Koper[13] proposed a model for the exchange of learning objects that suggests that it is important to construct certain use cases for building communities. We consider that images and their descriptive metadata are simple examples of learning objects, so it is worthwhile stating these use cases:

Key use cases to realise exchange from a technological perspective

- Find, get, edit and (dis)aggregate objects

- Upload version, upload new and add metadata

- Feedback and logging of use

- Communicate and collaborate

Key use cases to realise exchange of material in a community

- Needs assessment
- Manage and apply policies
  - IPR
  - Standardised terms and conditions of use

In order to build trust among community members, it is important from the outset to define roles for users within that community. There need to be *social moderators*, who are policy makers and upholders of the community's rules, and *facilitators*, who are active members with technical knowledge of the system and who provide support to other members and contributors. Both roles should be filled by members of the subject community who are aligned with their subject discipline and consider its needs from a subject-specific point of view. These users will already have knowledge of activity within their local sphere, department, research group, library or institution, broadening out to the national and international arena.

Bookplate of the Monmouth Parocial Library
© Andrew Prescott.

There are many excellent examples of community sites provided by the commercial sector, and the features and functions offered by the best of them should be incorporated into the visual directory.

Roles and responsibilities

Image-related services such as TASI and AHDS[14] Visual Arts should give technical support and advice to help collection providers integrate into the model.

HEA subject centres and data centres such as Archaeology Data Service should maintain the visual directory and provide specialist knowledge from the subject perspective.

The museum and heritage sectors, libraries and the Common Information Environment should act as partners to the subject centres.

The JISC Images Working Group, JISC Legal Advisory Team, OSS Watch and interoperability and metadata standards bodies such as CETIS should give guidance and direction to the subject centres.

The model requires very little in the way of central support staff, perhaps one or two people, with as much work as possible devolved to subject communities and stakeholders. This means time and effort should initially be spent on fostering social networking and on face-to-face meetings of providers. If implemented in this fashion the model should not cause long-term funding issues; stakeholders should receive additional funding to support community image collections, and grants could be awarded to the community to encourage them to donate material.

In this way the CLIC model would provide a valuable test bed of image material and resources that could be incorporated into further national repository work such as Jorum and institutional repositories. It could help aid the creation of e-learning materials and provide a use-case for portal work.

Hotel with a difference – medieval fortress, Parador Alarcon
© Linda Purdy.

Implementing the CLIC Model

There are four key stages to the implementation of the CLIC three-tier model. These are:

1. The social networking stage in which structures to support image sharing are formed

2. A call for material in which subject-based silos are created, by issuing small grants to community image providers

3. The catalogue-sharing stage: metadata is shared through photofeeds

4. National collections incorporate image-based material from the subject silos

Stage 1 – social networking stage

The foundation stage will use established communication methods and technologies to build communities among image providers.

- Social connections could be built up by means of an annual workshop or conference.

- Mailing lists to which interested parties can subscribe would be a low-cost way to gain access to individuals within institutions.

- Subject centres should be encouraged to provide information on the needs of their user communities.

- The visual directory should be expanded to become a 'MySpace'[15] directory of image providers, and include sample material and a free RSS photofeed alerting service.

This work lays the foundations for social interaction, which is a necessity for any collaborative work. Activity in this area increases the potential for cross-sector discovery of material and would also provide a user-led forum for discussion of requirements on standardisation of licences, file formats, metadata interchange etc. It may also produce an amount of Creative Commons-style material if providers wish to showcase material from their collections. A visual directory that has a subject-oriented interface will also help gauge the extent of coverage across the various subject areas. The technical needs of the first stage are relatively lightweight and can easily be achieved with off-the-shelf, freely available, open-source software:

- Wiki – suitable for providing a visual directory with sample image material

- Blog Server – suitable for providing news from the image-provider sites

- Bulletin Board – suitable for discussion of user needs and requirements

The visual directory would ideally be linked into the Information Environment Service Registry[16], which provides a method for computer systems, rather than humans, to access the directory. This integration may have to be deferred until a later stage, when sufficient catalogue material is available.

This stage has clearly defined goals that are achievable within a short timeframe and will build upon the work done for the CLIC study in identifying collections willing to participate in the visual directory.

Stage 2 – call for material

Small funding initiatives would be used to create small teaching-based silos of copyright-cleared images. These should be managed by stakeholders, such as the HEAs who already award grants to members of their subject communities. Images collected under these schemes should be subject to certain requirements:

- All material must be born digital or never previously published, and suitable for release under a Creative Commons-style licence

- All images should have complete catalogue data that can be expressed according to Dublin Core

- Images should be hosted by HEAs or other subject-based data centres, in a manner that would allow the images to be made available in Stage 3

The technical needs of this second stage are lightweight but the processes of cataloguing and the creation of descriptive metadata will be time-consuming and costly.

This stage requires a large amount of cross-sector activity:

- Short-term goal – set up a call for material

- Medium-term goal – host material at HEAs or subject data centres

- Long-term goal – metadata can be harvested

Stage 3 – catalogue-sharing activity

This stage will bring together the dispersed image collections by making use of metadata that has been exposed in the preceding stage. Initially, this would be done via RSS photofeeds, but could lead on to an Open Archive Initiative Procedure for Metadata Harvesting (OAI-PMH) system that has been adapted to support images and multimedia.

Reflections
© Lorraine Estelle.

Schemas already exist that would facilitate a pilot study to provide catalogue information expressed by means of Dublin Core and incorporate this information, together with a thumbnail image, into an RSS photofeed. These feeds could be aggregated by institutional consumers, subject-based portals and national services.

The OAI-PMH system would need to be adapted to provide the same functionality as is already possible with RSS and photofeeds but, in the longer term, it is likely that this modification would be of benefit to the OAI and image-provider communities by enabling better integration.

This stage provides an excellent opportunity for the repository community to give guidance to image providers on best practice in post-submission cataloguing in various subject areas.

Even a little progress on cataloguing would allow better facilities for cross-search and discovery of image material. There is significant benefit in educating image providers in appropriate use of metadata; work to extend the OAI-PMH would benefit both communities.

This stage could be difficult to implement, due to a lack of underlying catalogue exposure mechanisms in community collections, and difficult to fund and coordinate on a large scale.

Stage 4 – national collection activity

This final stage should be able to use images and catalogue material that has been produced in preceding stages. This material should be integrated with national initiatives such as portals and repositories that are currently being developed. Any proposed sound, image and multimedia portal, and learning object repositories such as Jorum, should aim to integrate with the CLIC model and incorporate material provided by communities into its own holdings.

This stage will also be difficult to implement. It involves coordinating activity across different sectors and performing technical interoperability work that may have little discernible result in the short term. If users' needs are to be met, there must be adequate consultation with the end-user communities.

The success of this stage will rely on integration with:

- National portal activity
- Learning Object repositories such as Jorum
- National collections in the museum and library sectors

Benefits

Technical considerations

According to our survey, collection providers do not have the technical knowledge, time or money to implement up-coming technical solutions such as the OAI-PMH, Search/Retrieve via the Web (SRW)[17] or Shibboleth. It is unlikely that collection providers will seek to implement these technologies unless they can demonstrate real value. It is much more likely that image providers will be able and willing to implement simple, well-understood, proven technologies such as RSS photofeeds and Dublin Core metadata. The CLIC model seeks to build upon the adoption of these technologies to implement more sophisticated technical solutions currently under development.

The CLIC study identified archiving of content as a technical requirement that collection providers feel to be of value. Repositories and subject silos should consider offering an archival service as a way of encouraging image collections to contribute their material. Similarly, the subject silos should implement solutions such as OAI-PMH and SRW for their holdings and actively encourage collection providers to implement the same technologies. This would best be achieved if software libraries implementing some of these technologies were developed in a variety of programming languages and maintained by advisory services such as TASI or AHDS Visual Arts.

Ensuring 'buy-in' by the community

It is generally considered that providing high-quality material is not enough to guarantee that resources are used. They must be perceived as meeting the needs of users. A recent review of digital repositories work[18] concluded:

> *Repository interfaces should be directed towards 'communities of practice' and more effort should be made to tailor services for specific user communities, rather than producing generic interfaces. This is likely to be particularly important to encourage take-up within FE, although it is still important with HE... Repository developments should, depending upon their primary focus, relate to the processes and practices of research, teaching or learning – buy-in from the community is unlikely to be extensive unless this happens. JISC should identify current practice of researchers, teachers and learners, and seek to base services on supporting their needs.*

It has also been suggested by the JISC Exchange for Learning Programme (X4L) manager, investigating re-purposing and sharing of existing and forthcoming content, that teaching and learning repositories need to focus on delivering to 'communities of practice' if significant take-up and use of the content is to be achieved.

Penguins
© Seamus Ross.

Benefits of subject-based, community-led collections

The Rights and Rewards academic survey[19] found that people generally turn to their nearest neighbours when looking for support materials and that the most active support is given to subject-based repositories rather than generic or institutional ones. CLIC found that image providers were similarly inclined to support for the idea of donating material to subject-based repositories.

Most of the more successful image collections, such as the BioScience Imagebank, and medical image collections, such as the Wellcome Trust's Medical Photographic Library, are based on specific-subject disciplines; even SCRAN[20] (Scottish Cultural Resources Access Network) was originally focused on Scottish culture. Throughout its study, CLIC found that subject-based and community collections had already had some exposure, within relevant subject fields, and were better known than generic collections or collections based around subjects that differed from the respondent's own expertise.

With this in mind, we feel it is important that any model supports communities in their efforts to organise and help themselves and is, as far as possible, open access. Key factors that support choosing a subject-centred model include:

- Increased likelihood of community submission and sharing
- Increased relevance of material and appropriateness of metadata
- Ownership and trust
- Common goals and values
- Long-term sustainability
- Existing archival activities
- Existing funding structures and strands

In order for a subject-based model such as we propose to succeed, it must contain material that is useful to the communities it is intended to serve. This can be achieved by incorporating material created by a community of practice into a collection from the outset.

Summary of CLIC findings

The CLIC study considers that local needs are best met locally, with support from subject-based communities of practice to provide a core of copyright-cleared material. National initiatives should be driven by subject-based demand. Community-owned repositories, containing material in their own right, would provide subject-based points of access to relevant material in local and national collections.

Bodies acting as subject specialists should work to build up small corpuses of teaching material. A register of visual teaching material needs and requirements should be established as soon as possible.

Life guards, St. Ives, Cornwall
© Mike Pringle. Photograph.

Communities of practice need to be identified and nurtured until they are mature. Ideally, this would be done through subject specialists who are well qualified and best placed to undertake the task. Nominated liaison contacts and mailing lists need to be set up and coordinated by the subject centre HEAs, Intute, TASI and national initiatives such as the AHDS. However, communities must feel that they, and not national institutions, are the owners of their collections. There is motivation for people to donate material if the structures are open and clear.

Creative Commons licences, or a limited number of Creative Commons-style licences, should be adopted as the default licensing system for born-digital, nationally funded initiatives. These must always accompany the images and could dispel the miasma of confusion over IPR that prevents the sharing and modification of material.

A series of community-owned directories of image collections, in which collections would register themselves, should be set up immediately as a first step towards coordinating future cooperation within communities. After initial seeding, these should be maintained and supported by the communities with minimal system administration.

Partnerships for sharing subject material must be explored across the education, museum and commercial sectors at national and international levels.

The three-tiered model being proposed assumes that there is interoperability among levels and across subjects via metadata cross-searching or aggregation. This would be a challenge to implement within a distributed, community-owned structure and we did not see underlying infrastructure mechanisms in existing community image collections. While efforts should be made to ensure compatibility, it may prove more efficient to concentrate on more lightweight discovery mechanisms, such as RSS/RDF, that are already in widespread use and could readily be adopted by community image collections.

References

1. TASI (Technical Advisory Service for Images): provides guidance and advice to the education sector on the use of image material
http://www.tasi.ac.uk/

2. Resource Discovery Network *See also* Intute
http://www.rdn.ac.uk/

3. Intute
http://www.intute.ac.uk/

4. EMBL (European Molecular Biology Laboratories)
http://www.ebi.ac.uk/embl/

5. Dublin Core metadata initiative: provides a minimal set of metadata terms that can be used to categorise most types of material
http://dublincore.org/

6. Creative Commons Licences
http://creativecommons.org/

7. *the* Digital Picture; a UK-wide initiative to explore digital image issues in the visual arts education community
http://www.thedigitalpicture.ac.uk/

8. Creative Archive, a collaboration between the BBC, the British Film Institute, Channel 4 and the Open University
http://creativearchive.bbc.co.uk/

9. CIE (Common Information Environment) group,
http://www.common-info.org.uk,
A report on the use of Creative Common licences across a range of UK publicly funded organizations
http://www.jisc.ac.uk/index.cfm?name=wg_cie_home

10. Jorum, an online repository service for teaching and support staff in UK further and higher education institutions
http://www.jorum.ac.uk/

11. HEA (Higher Education Academies)
http://www.heacademy.ac.uk/

12. Wikipedia, an online user-contributed encyclopedia
http://wikipedia.org/

13. Koper, R. et al., 2004. Building communities for the exchange of learning objects: theoretical foundation and requirements, *ALT-J, Research in Learning Technology*, vol. 12, no. 1

14. AHDS (Arts and Humanities Data Service)
http://ahds.ac.uk/

15. Myspace, an online community site
http://www.myspace.com/

16. Information Environment Service Registry – a system to allow applications to discover and use materials which will help their users' learning, teaching and research
http://iesr.ac.uk/

17. Search/Retrieve via the Web (SRW), a system for returning search results from archives via web services
http://www.loc.gov/standards/sru/

18. Heery, R. and Anderson, S., 2005, Digital Repositories Review
http://www.jisc.ac.uk/uploaded_documents/digital-repositories-review-2005.pdf

19. Bates, M., Gadd, E., Loddington, S., Manuel, S., & Oppenheim, C., 2006. Rights and Rewards in Blended Institutional Repositories Project. *ALISS Quarterly*, 1(3), 47-51

20. SCRAN, a long-established charity providing images and multimedia to education
http://www.scran.ac.uk/

Further reading

CHERRI-Pie
http://www.cherri.mvm.ed.ac.uk/

Enrich UK, gateway to lottery-funded online collections
http://www.enrichuk.net/

Flickr, an online tool for storing, searching, and organizing photographs
http://www.flickr.com/

Gordon Conference, Visualisation in Science Education
http://community.middlebury.edu/~grc/

Internet Archive
http://www.archive.org/

JISC Digital Repository and Supporting Digital Preservation and Asset
Management in Institutions programmes
http://www.jisc.ac.uk/index.cfm?name=programme_digital_repositories

JISC Information Environment
http://www.jisc.ac.uk/index.cfm?name=ie_home

Lave, J and Wenger, E. (1991). *Situated Learning – Legitimate Peripheral
Participation*, Cambridge University Press

Museums, Libraries and Archives Council
http://www.mla.gov.uk/

Open Archives Initiative
http://www.openarchives.org/community/index.html

Rights and Rewards study, Loughborough University January 2006, funded
under the JISC Digital Repositories Programme
http://rightsandrewards.lboro.ac.uk/

Wikicommons, an online store of user-contributed, copyright-cleared media file
for use in the wikipedia project
http://commons.wikimedia.org/

Chapter 5

Towards a Clinical Commons: Using Clinical Recordings in Academic Non-Clinical Settings

Rachel Ellaway, Helen Cameron and Michael Ross with contributions from Graeme Laurie, Margaret Maxwell and Rebekah Pratt

Images from clinical recordings are crucial to education in a number of fields, but restrictions on their use are many.

Towards a Clinical Commons: Using Clinical Recordings in Academic Non-Clinical Settings

http://www.cherri.mvm.ed.ac.uk

Images and other recordings created in clinical settings are, for obvious reasons, difficult to share. There are the ethical issues, often relating to when and how to get permission to re-use the image in an educational context, and there are the legal issues in ensuring that the owners of the image have their rights protected. Following high-profile cases in which confidential medical information has been inadvertently released, there can be reluctance even to discuss the use of clinical images in non-clinical (i.e. educational) settings, but this poses serious risks. For one thing, a lack of legitimate access to such images may well impact on the training of health professionals. The work begun by the study reported in this chapter is a significant further step on the road to an infrastructure that will mean that:

- patients will be assured that images of them or their relatives will only be used according to the permissions they have granted, for as long as this permission is granted

- clinicians and allied professionals will be assured that the images they create can be used to improve medical training, but that they will be used only for defined purposes

- educators will be assured that they can use clinical images, confident that they have the demonstrable right to do so

As the authors of this chapter acknowledge, the consent and licensing model put forward is only a start, and needs to be both developed by a broad range of stakeholders and supplemented by tools so that it can be implemented. The model, and allied strands of work, mark an important and timely opportunity, for example, as the UK National Health Service continues to move toward an integrated and digital information environment.

Neil Jacobs
JISC Programme Manager

Introduction

The use of clinical recordings such as images, videos, audio recordings, scans, test results and patient notes has been a fundamental part of healthcare education for decades. More recently, however, the development of digital and internet technologies has significantly altered the way these materials can be used, reused, transported, copied and stored. These changes have influenced the social and ethical dimensions of personal information, which has in turn led to developments in the law and professional guidance regulating the use of such recordings.

The same technological developments that have contributed to a tightening of the law regarding their use have also led to a rethinking of ownership, collaboration and access to information, in both clinical and more general contexts. In the last few years the reuse of digital content has been the focus of both European and UK investment as manifested in the development of repositories of digital educational content and standards and specifications to describe and manage them. Shared digital materials for healthcare education have been the focus of a number of projects and services, but because of the clinical origin of many of these recordings there remains a great deal of uncertainty about whether and how they may be shared.

Despite UK-wide data protection and human rights legislation, and guidance from bodies such as the General Medical Council (GMC), current practice regarding the acquisition and use of clinical recordings for academic non-clinical settings (CRANCS) in the UK is highly varied. Following concerns about this the UK Joint Information Systems Committee (JISC) in 2005 commissioned a team from the University of Edinburgh to investigate the area and provide recommendations for developing practice. The resulting project was called CHERRI (Common Healthcare Educational Recordings Reusability Infrastructure)[1], and this chapter outlines its main findings. Copies of the full report and other supporting documents can be obtained from the CHERRI project website at www.cherri.mvm.ed.ac.uk.

The survey and interviews undertaken by CHERRI revealed that most practitioners were aware of relevant legislation and national guidance relating to patient consent and confidentiality, but did not know how to translate these into processes in the local context, where images would often be acquired in a clinical setting but used in an educational one. For some the process stops at acquiring informed consent and recordings, a few try to log subsequent usage, but many, faced with uncertainty and risk, are turning away from the use of CRANCS altogether. The uncertainty in practice did not only relate to consent, as many practitioners were also unclear about issues of ownership and copyright.

Problems identified included a lack of common process and standards at a local level, a lack of connection between terms of consent and subsequent use, unnecessary duplication of recordings, consent and guidance in local contexts as a safety measure, and a pervading culture of risk and uncertainty that is leading to both individual and institutional anxiety and loss of utility.

Current UK legal framework and guidelines

The key legal concepts invoked by the use of CRANCS in the UK are those of consent, privacy and property. Different legal regulatory regimes, and thus legal liabilities and remedies, apply depending upon which rights and interests are in play. Consent for CRANCS should probably be of a higher standard than that of what a 'prudent patient' would require to give informed consent for treatment (as, unlike in clinical care, there is little potential benefit for the patient) and is governed by the common law remedies of negligence (if participants suffer demonstrable harm) and breach of confidence (for unauthorised uses of data), as well as some aspects of the Data Protection Act (1998)[2]. Privacy is mostly protected by the Human Rights Act (1998)[3], Article 8 'Respect for private and family life', and the Data Protection Act (1998), although the common law duty of confidentiality also applies. Various regimes of property law apply, including database rights, which declare that control, use and extractions belong to the database owner, and copyright, which gives ownership to the creator of the recording. The subject of a recording usually has no claim of property on that recording, but could seek legal remedy through one of the above (e.g. privacy), through defamation if adverse inferences may be drawn about the subject or through breach of contract if one exists. Various other legal concepts may be invoked depending upon the situation, such as the Freedom of Information Act (2000)[4], Freedom of Information (Scotland) Act (2002)[5], Mental Capacity Act (2005)[6], Age of Legal Capacity (Scotland) Act (1991)[7], Access to Health Records Act (1990)[8], Telecommunications Act (1984)[9] and Adults with Incapacity (Scotland) Act (2000)[10]. There is considerable potential for conflict between the rights and interests of the various parties involved, and it is important to appreciate how such tensions might arise and how they might be resolved.

In the 1990s the Caldicott Committee reviewed all patient-identifiable information (including clinical recordings) passing out of National Health Service organisations for purposes other than direct care, with the purpose of minimising unnecessary information transfer. Its report[11] highlighted many of the issues surrounding CRANCS and recommended clear guidelines and protocols for the management of such information. The Department of Health has since issued a reference guide to consent for examination or treatment[12] and an implementation guide[13], the NHS code of practice on confidentiality[14] and the NHS code of practice for records management[15]. Complementing this guidance are General Medical Council publications on the creation and use of patient recordings[16], consent[17] and confidentiality[18]; the Institute of Medical Illustrators code of practice[19] and model policy and procedure[20]and the British Medical Association guidance on the creation and use of patient recordings[21]. Various other professional bodies have issued guidance around the creation and use of CRANCS, please see References [22,23]. and [24]. A full synthesis and discussion of the guidance based around the GMC 2002 document can be found in the CHERRI report and has been summarised below:

- **General principles:** Seek appropriate consent (as described in GMC 1998) for recordings, ensuring that patients understand enough about the nature and purposes of the recording to make an informed decision and do not feel pressurised. Do not use recordings for purposes outside this without further consent. Stop or do not record if the patient asks, if the recording is having an adverse affect on their clinical care, or if it compromises their privacy or dignity. The minimum required information should be passed only to those who need to know (and extraneous information should be removed). Appropriate security arrangements should be made for the storage of recordings, which should be destroyed if consent for use is withdrawn or the recording is no longer required.

- **Apparently anonymous recordings made for clinical purposes (such as radiological recordings, those of internal organs or during laparoscopy, and small external areas of the subject such as small skin lesions):** Most authorities suggest that if such clinical recordings are truly anonymous (or have been 'anonymised' by removal of personal identifiers), then no further consent is required to use them for non-clinical purposes except publication. However, some authorities feel that consent should be obtained for all CRANCS, whether identifiable or not, as it is impossible to know what apparently minor details may be used to identify the subject of a recording.

- **Apparently identifiable recordings made for clinical purposes:** Appropriate consent should be obtained in all cases unless otherwise specified below.

- **Recordings made for non-clinical purposes:** All recordings of patients taken in a clinical context form part of their medical records; appropriate consent should be obtained in all cases, and a copy of the recording should be stored in the patient record. This does not apply if the recordings occur outside a healthcare context (i.e. if the subjects are not 'patients').

Patients should not be exposed to unnecessary risks for non-clinical purposes such as X-rays.

- **Historical collections and those arising outside the UK:** Recordings in which a patient may be identifiable should not be used for teaching purposes if appropriate consent cannot be demonstrated. Recordings made for teaching purposes prior to 1997 in which the patient is not identifiable and no consent is available may be used until suitable replacement recordings can be made. It is also important to consider whether consent is still valid for the suggested use of the recording.

- **Recordings of incapacitated adults:** This usually requires careful consideration by experts in consultation with next-of-kin relatives and significant others. If a patient is temporarily incapacitated (e.g. under anaesthetic) and an exceptional unplanned opportunity for recording arises, some state that this may be undertaken, but appropriate consent must be sought from the patient on recovery; however the area is contentious as the recordings could not usually be justified in terms of necessity in the patient's best interests.

- **Recordings of children:** Patients over 16, and those under 16 who have capacity to make an informed decision (in Scotland determined by the Age of Legal Capacity (Scotland) Act 1991)can make their own decisions about making and using CRANCS. Parents or guardians can usually make decisions on behalf of children under 16 who lack capacity, but the wishes of the child should be sought and recordings should not be made if the child disagrees. The area of non-accidental injury recordings is particularly complex and should always involve experts.

- **Recordings of telephone calls:** Anyone using a telephone is subject to the Telecommunications Act 1984, which disallows covert recordings except under exceptional conditions.

- **Recordings for use in public and broadcast media:** With few exceptions, patients' express consent should be obtained for each use of a clinical recording in the public domain. Such recordings should as far as possible exclude all identifiable information.

- **Recordings of patients who have died:** Next-of-kin relatives can usually make decisions about post-mortem recordings, and in exceptional circumstances may be approached for consent to use recordings taken in life, but if similar recordings can be made and appropriately consented from live patients this is preferable.

Current UK practice

The CHERRI project studied current UK practice using an online questionnaire, a request for information to Caldicott guardians and heads of medical schools, and qualitative telephone interviews to key stakeholders in the creation and use of CRANCS.

There were 38 returns to the online questionnaire, 71% of which reported having procedures for dealing with consent for CRANCS; 66% had paper-based consent forms and 56% reported no limits of time or location in consenting for CRANCS. 48% reported that subjects received written information about the use of recordings during the consent process (although only 32% and 6% gave subjects a copy of the consent form and recording respectively) and 42% reported that access to CRANCS obtained in their institution would be limited to their own staff. 32% reported that they were not aware of any guidelines around CRANCS and only 11% reported using guidelines in all situations. In addition to the questionnaire, a request for information was sent to all Caldicott Guardians (620 senior staff in the NHS and social services appointed to protect patient information) and heads of medical schools (31) in the UK asking for any guidelines, protocols or consent forms relating to CRANCS. There were only 35 returns to this request (a response rate of just over 5%) – 19 reporting that they could not send anything (seven Strategic Health Authorities, five using outside sources of guidance, six reporting having none and one declining to participate), six sent variations of the DOH model consent form, two sent variations on the IMI model documents and eight others sent documentation of variable content and quality. There are various potential reasons why the responses to the questionnaire and information request were so poor, including apprehension or discomfort about CRANCS (an issue highlighted in the qualitative interviews) and a failure to recognise that the request for copies of relevant current guidance fell within the scope of the Freedom of Information Act 2000.

A qualitative interview sampling frame was created to ensure representation of different organisations, roles, professions and patient groups from across the UK; and an interview schedule was developed to explore the five main themes of background and involvement with CRANCS, guidelines, consent, data tracking, storage and access, and future concerns. 24 qualitative telephone interviews were conducted with medical educators, illustrators, publishers, clinicians, shared resource representatives, veterinarian educators and patient representatives. The main findings are summarised as follows.

- **Background.** There is a perceived increase in public awareness and changing social attitudes towards the production and use of CRANCS. There is a great deal of uncertainty and fear of litigation around the production and use of CRANCS, leading to some trying to minimise their use or avoid using them altogether.

- **Guidelines.** There is great variety in the role of guidelines and policies to guide practice. Knowledge of external policies is variable (with the GMC being most influential). The absence of internal policies is often justified through the use of common sense, consent forms and reference to external policies.

- **Consent.** Most are satisfied with their own consent policy but many suggest that it is difficult to assess how well their policy is working. Most have consent forms, which reflect the wide variety of practices (ranging from broad general consent to specific consent relating to medical notes, education and publication). Consent is usually not limited by time or geography. Consent for publication seems to be particularly challenging with the rise of electronic publication, particularly of academic and professional journals.

- **Data tracking, storage and access.** Small, informal data-storage systems are common. The use of database management of images is growing in use, and it seems the more organised a system of storage is, the easier it is to manage access securely, and the more efficiently issues of withdrawing consent can be managed.

- **Future concerns.** Shared resources are appealing for many, although they perceive a range of difficulties to overcome in relation to developing a successful shared resource. National guidelines would be welcomed as a way to clarify practice and raise awareness about the issues around the non-clinical use of clinical images. Emerging technologies (such as mobile phones with cameras) continue to challenge policy and practice, and as such future developments will need to be accommodated in any legal and practical frameworks and policies.

Towards a common framework for practice

There appears, at the time of writing, to be widespread understanding of the principles and legal framework that should guide the acquisition and use of CRANCS, but there is also an appreciation of the limitations of current guidance and the need to work towards a common process or framework, particularly if the use of CRANCS is to be developed locally or as a shared resource. There are a number of factors regarding the use of CRANCS that need to be accommodated in any common framework:

- Informed consent needs to be acquired, although further clarification is needed on the extent to which express consent is required for all recordings, either as a legal requirement or as a professional code of practice. Changes in the use of a recording will most likely require additional consent.

- The opportunity to acquire relevant images usually arises from patients' attendance at NHS services, predominantly a general practice surgery or hospital, and the NHS also resources the acquisition of such images and claims copyright. With appropriate consent, images are transferred from the NHS to further or higher education institutions; seldom the other way. In the case of animals, it is usually the veterinary surgeon providing care who arranges for images to be procured. Healthcare organisations are familiar with the legal framework and guidance around consent, confidentiality and use of health data. They currently not only have systems for obtaining consent and filing the relevant documentation in patient records, they also undertake dissemination of explanatory material through booklets, posters and letters as to when and how patient data and images might be used.

- The terms of consent need to be provided with and attached to the recording so that they can be made available to any subsequent user. The key linking the recording and terms of consent with details of the individual patient would remain with the originator of the recording (ideally within the NHS).

- Without making available any personal information, there needs to be a persistent and unique link between a recording and the identity of the patient who has given consent for it. This would provide an audit trail and a process for managing procedures such as withdrawal of consent, or requests for further consent to use recordings for other purposes.

- These procedures should be undertaken by all users of CRANCS to ensure a common basis for using and reusing them. As global implementation is unlikely in the short term, efforts should be made within specific communities to ensure adoption and use of common frameworks which could over time align to form a single framework.

- The acquisition of consent is not in itself sufficient, as there are also aspects of ownership and conditions of use that are not found in the consent process and must be addressed in addition to it. Consent is nonetheless essential for any material that is identifiable and often advisable even when it is not.

- If patient consent is not required (e.g. for non-identifiable recordings) there remains a need to identify provenance and copyright and make an affirmative recorded statement that explicit consent is not required for the academic use of that particular recording.

Consent and licensing models

Licensing is in effect a form of contract between the provider and all subsequent users and it can encapsulate any conditions of use that the licensor wishes and the licensee agrees to. In this way consent and copyrights can be managed together. While basic copyright is enshrined in national law (with variations between jurisdictions), licensing, as a form of contract, can add or remove conditions from basic copyright and can act as a common trans-jurisdictional rights framework.

Most published material is currently provided under specific licences – for instance the end-user licences (EULs) displayed when a software package is installed or a video played. One model currently attracting a lot of attention is Creative Commons[25]. Creative Commons (CC) is based on just six basic licences, each of which is recast in the legal language of individual jurisdictions worldwide. Although the wording of the full licences is different in each jurisdiction, the global conditions remain the same. This means that materials licensed under CC can be used under the same conditions anywhere in the world that has a CC licensing structure.

Despite the growing popularity and evident simplicity of CC, there are many specific problems for its use with CRANCS:

- Once granted, CC use is forever – this is contrary to data protection, which requires use for no longer than necessary and is certainly contrary to any idea of withdrawal of consent and therefore of use

- Once granted, CC use is everywhere – this is potentially contrary to data protection, which prohibits transfer of personal information outside the EU except where there are equivalent data protection regulations

- There is no concept of patient consent in CC, only copyright

Alternatives to a licensing model might be to improve practice through dissemination of current best practice and the principles of informed consent along with the promotion of a common consent form and process. The first two must certainly go hand in hand with longer term plans to create a common framework for the use of CRANCS and are to be supported for their simplicity and low cost, but they are unlikely to address many of the issues raised in this project.

As described above it is usually healthcare providers who arrange for images to be recorded to support clinical management and/or for use in teaching and research; and it is in the clinical setting that consent for future uses of images is sought, logged and stored in the patient record along with a copy of the image. The NHS is expert at obtaining and safeguarding patient-identifiable data and images, is well versed in the legal and professional requirements, and has a duty and opportunity to explain to patients through personal and public information systems how their data and images might be used. The consent and acquisition processes should therefore remain within the NHS to serve the patients' interests and acknowledge the NHS claim of copyright on all images originating from clinical care.

However, images are increasingly being passed on to institutions of further and higher education to illustrate PowerPoint lecture slides and online teaching packages, and here there is a risk that the conditions of use will immediately be lost. A paper copy of the consent form is likely to be the best source of information currently sent with an image, but this practice is unwieldy, with problems of storage and transfer, and risks making the image even more identifiable as the consent form passes to every system administrator. Institutions of education do not have a long tradition of storing such sensitive personal material amongst their learning resources and, as seen in the CHERRI interviews, few staff could confidently explain where and how consent would be stored in their local education centre.

This simple model of consent travelling with the image fails to make the conditions of consent apparent to users, so will not limit inappropriate copying, changing or use in other contexts. It also does little to improve recall of images. Without metadata, searching for a specific image recalled at a patient's request may be like looking for a needle in a haystack. The alternative would be complex logging of use attached to the education centre's copy of the consent form.

A simple system relying only on registered consent is less obvious to staff and students, thereby running the risk of being overlooked and unevenly adopted; without protocol-driven practice it will be very difficult to encourage all staff to safeguard patients' interests and without metadata there will be no obvious signal that teaching and assessment resources had been legitimately acquired and used.

A common framework of practice must therefore address both the consent and contract requirements for the use of CRANCS. The term 'Clinical

Commons' has been adopted for the proposed licensing regime, based on the simplicity and trans-jurisdictional nature of Creative Commons but specifically accommodating the needs of the clinical community. The 'Science Commons', arising out of genetic research, has created a precedent for adaptive models based on Creative Commons, and provisional discussions have taken place with Creative Commons and their affiliates in the UK with respect to Clinical Commons, though no definite decision or action had taken place at the time of writing.

The model for Clinical Commons also draws heavily on the operation of the Health Education Assets Library (HEAL) in the USA. Consent procedures vary between states, but there is a single federal act that unifies all states with a set of procedures governing the transfer of personal patient information. This legislation is called the Health Insurance Portability and Accountability Act 1996 (HIPAA)[26] and HEAL requires all depositors to sign an HIPAA declaration that their materials have been properly consented. Thus the physician (or his/her proxy) undertakes the consent and takes responsibility for it by ensuring it follows HIPAA requirements. This effectively indemnifies HEAL against action regarding holding personal information in the form of clinical images.

The recommended procedure for Clinical Commons combines a consent and licensing step to create a properly consented resource that can then be released to the academic community and beyond with its conditions of use clearly described for all to see. This two-phase process is shown in Figure 5.1:

Figure 5.1
The CHERRI Consent and Licensing (C+L) Model.

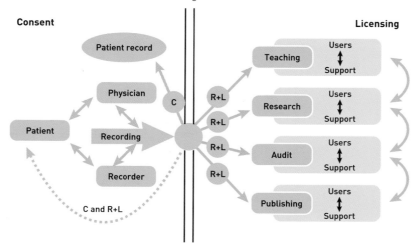

This illustrates a situation where a patient (possibly with their guardian or other family members) is seen by a physician who requests that a recording is taken. The consent is taken either by the physician or the recorder (who might be a medical photographer or the physician). A licence is drawn up and signed by a responsible staff member, regardless of the need for explicit consent, and is made available along with the recording for non-clinical use. For images requiring explicit consent the licence is linked to the consent in perpetuity through use of a shared globally unique identifier (GUID) which encodes the identity of the patient and is maintained securely by the healthcare provider. The licence describes the copyright conditions along with either a declaration that consent is not required or a description of the conditions of consent. Within each use context there may be those who use the recording (such as teachers) or those who support users (such as technical staff). Because the recording and its licence (R+L) are not separated, they can be passed from one use context to another with impunity, as the conditions under which the recording can be used are known and expressed in a commonly understood format. In addition the consent (C), recording and/or licence can be entered into the patient record or made available to the patient.

The CHERRI Consent and Licensing (C+L) Model ensures that consent and the resulting documentation stay within the health-service provider. Use of a globally unique identifier (GUID) would be recorded on the licence and consent form to enable reconciliation at a later date if required (for instance in support of withdrawal of consent by the patient or the copyright owner).

A CRANCS life cycle can be drawn incorporating a common consent and licensing process as follows:

- **Evaluation:** Current guidelines on when consent is and is not required are commonly available to all healthcare practitioners, though further clarification on what constitutes 'non-identifiable' images may be required.

- **Acquisition:** The acquisition of consent is structured to ensure that all anticipated uses are discussed with patients and to enable a common format for expression of the conditions of consent. The consent (or declaration that consent is not required) and copyright conditions are rendered in a commonly formatted licence, which can be attached to the recording in different ways (depending on the form/medium of the recording). The licence and consent are given a common unique ID. The latter is stored in the patient record in a way that makes the licence ID subsequently searchable. The patient would be given a copy of the licence and/or consent along with information on how to withdraw consent later if desired, and may also be given a copy of the recording.

- **Storage:** The recording is stored with its licence. This may take the form of an XML file or database entry in a repository or equivalent system that allows the licence conditions to be exposed as part of a search for resources. In-recording licence marks such as icons, by-lines or other marks are part of the recording itself but not necessarily discoverable in a search. Access to CRANCS can be limited to users with suitable qualifications or recorded at the point of access. Metadata may also record different applications or uses of the CRANCS. The pairing of the CRANCS with its licence is supported by different storage systems.

- **Usage:** The CRANCS are made available to users along with the terms of use. Practitioners will refuse to use CRANCS that do not have an attached licence as lacking sufficient provenance. Artefacts created using CRANCS will display the conditions of use of all constituent CRANCS and the use of the artefact will be governed by the combined conditions of use of all CRANCS along with any licensing or restrictions associated with the artefact as a whole.

- **Policy and community building:** By instituting a common model for the use of CRANCS, all associated activity in different institutions, professions and sectors can be normalised (at least to some extent) and both patients and practitioners better supported and protected from inadvertent risk.

- **Maintenance and termination:** By exposing licence metadata and using a persistent and trackable unique licence ID that is paired with the patient record in the cases of explicit consent, withdrawal requests can be more easily met, conditions of use monitored and accountability more clearly established. There will be times when it will not be possible to withdraw all copies of a recording, for instance in books, journals or online; in these cases all reasonable steps to withdraw recordings and prevent subsequent use should be taken.

Conclusions

The law and guidance on the use of CRANCS from professional and statutory bodies set out to protect the interests of patients, and generally practitioners are aware of the underpinning principles. However, local protocols do not take into account the explosion in the quality and mobility of digitised images. As a result, current practice in the creation, use and reuse of CRANCS is generally non-standardised, thereby creating risks and uncertainty for all concerned.

It's difficult to create a completely safe environment for the use of CRANCS without sacrificing their utility or aspects of a 'greater good'. Prohibiting the use of CRANCS for teaching and research would undermine the effectiveness of both and could have a significantly detrimental impact on the competence of future healthcare professionals. Furthermore, seeking explicit consent for all images is impractical but current public opinion and the law favour the rights of the individual patient, and standardised practices must take account of that, although there are differences of opinion in this area (Academy of Medical Sciences 2006[27]).

A common activity framework is required to support the acquisition, storage and use of CRANCS. Indeed it is absolutely essential for any large-scale and dynamic exchange of these kinds of recordings. Without greater normalisation of procedures, the continued use of CRANCS will create further risks and problems for individual patients and staff and for institutions and is likely to result in loss of utilitarian benefits. Such a framework has several important components.

Guidance on consent must continue to be updated to reflect changing social values and legal concerns about the use of CRANCS. It must continue to clarify for practitioners the situations in which explicit consent is required for images and the way in which they can address patients' reasonable expectations that they be kept informed about all uses of their data and images, including non-identifiable materials. Dissemination of best practice to aid the creation of standard consent procedures and documentation at a local level should address some of the concerns raised by practitioners.

It is also essential that a robust, simple-to-use and commonly acknowledged mechanism for handling consent with respect to clinical recordings is adopted across the UK. The CHERRI common consent and licensing model is proposed to address the problems. Based on the simplicity of Creative Commons it seeks to accommodate specific clinical responsibilities and issues.

The challenge now is to disseminate these proposals and develop them in consultation with key stakeholders in the tertiary education sector, the health service and professional bodies towards the implementation of a practical and efficient common set of processes. As the healthcare environment is subject to frequent change, the framework will inevitably require review and updating over time. Undertaking the work is not currently within any organisation's remit, although it may be of interest to a number of educational and healthcare bodies. Arrangements will need to be made to monitor the situation and action adjustments over time as and when they are required.

Recommendations

- That guidance from the GMC and other professional bodies on the use of patient recordings for teaching and research should continue to be regularly updated to take account of changing public and societal attitudes and concerns about use of CRANCS. The situations requiring explicit consent may change over time and even now further clarification is required around consent for 'non-identifiable images'.

- That all creators and users of CRANCS should be better educated and supported in the use of such recordings, and that this training and support should be normalised as much as possible both for quality assurance and economies of scale purposes.

  - This requires that complacency about current practices in obtaining and recording consent, and the use of images without knowledge that consent has been obtained, is robustly challenged.

  - Further work must be undertaken in consultation with all relevant and interested parties to develop a consensus view on recommendations for practice and the production of common national (and preferably international) guidelines and documentation for gaining consent for clinical recordings.

  - The appropriate technical infrastructure should be adopted pending further guidance, along with clear procedures for gaining consent, storage, sharing and withdrawal of clinical recordings.

  - Once national procedures and guidance are adopted, these should be publicised as widely as possible to professionals involved with CRANCS and also to the lay public. This will require adequate investment in appropriate training and in promoting the use of these guidelines.

- That a common consent and licence model for CRANCS is developed and adopted UK-wide (and preferably also in other jurisdictions, although the practicalities of this would need to be explored further).

- That any model adopted in the UK adheres to UK/European law and encompasses both consent and Intellectual Property Right dimensions of a recording.

- That the licensing model, Clinical Commons, is based on Creative Commons and set up and run either by CC or a qualified agency. There is an issue of jurisdiction here. The most useful model would be truly international with local rendering (as per Creative Commons) and as such a trans-national organisation such as Creative Commons would seem to be the logical home. However, it may be that medico-legal concerns would require management of a C+L model to be at a national level and undertaken by a responsible NGO such as the NHS in the UK.

- That all CRANCS are tagged (potentially visibly) with a C+L mark or icon to indicate their provenance and conditions of use. This icon should represent the different forms of use at a small enough resolution not to interfere with the recording.

- That practitioners refuse to use non-C+L materials because they lack sufficient provenance and guarantee of patients' interests. This clearly illustrates the compliance rather than enforcement nature of the approach, but the current environment and the availability of resources mean that an enforcement approach is impractical.

- That any central repository must adhere to the C+L model before any clinical materials are stored there. This combines issues of technical infrastructure, community-specific requirements and appropriate workflows. A national repository service like JORUM would need to accommodate the additional metadata, access controls and workflows associated with C+L to safely store and supply access to CRANCS. This may indicate that separate systems are required for CRANCS with access limited to healthcare education and its affiliates.

- That all relevant agencies have input to and support the development of this common model and that steps are taken to develop the relationship between the health service and the tertiary education sector.

References

1. CHERRI (Common Healthcare Educational Recordings Reusability Infrastructure). The full report is available online:
http://www.cherri.mvm.ed.ac.uk/cherri.pdf
The project website is:
http://www.cherri.mvm.ed.ac.uk/

2. Data Protection Act 1998. HMSO. Available online:
http://www.hmso.gov.uk/acts/acts1998/19980029.htm

3. Human Rights Act 1998. HMSO. Available online:
http://www.hmso.gov.uk/acts/acts1998/19980042.htm

4. Freedom of Information Act; 2000. HMSO. Available online:
http://www.hmso.gov.uk/acts/acts2000/20000036.htm

5. Freedom of Information (Scotland) Act; 2002.
http://www.hmso.gov.uk/legislation/scotland/acts2002/20020013.htm

6. Mental Capacity Act 2005. HMSO. Available online:
http://www.opsi.gov.uk/acts/acts2005/20050009.htm

7. Age of Legal Capacity (Scotland) Act 1991 (c.50). HMSO. Available online:
http://www.hmso.gov.uk/acts/acts1991/Ukpga_19910050_en_1.htm

8. Access to Health Records Act 1990 (c.23). HMSO. Available online:
   http://www.opsi.gov.uk/acts/acts1990/Ukpga_19900023_en_1.htm

9. Telecommunications Act 1984. HMSO. No longer available online.

10. Adults with Incapacity (Scotland) Act 2000. HMSO. Available online:
    http://www.opsi.gov.uk/legislation/scotland/acts2000/20000004.htm

11. DOH 1997. *The Caldicott Committee: Report on the review of patient-identifiable information.*
    Available online:
    http://www.dh.gov.uk/assetRoot/04/06/84/04/04068404.pdf

12. DOH 2001a. *Reference guide to consent for examination or treatment.* Available online:
    http://www.dh.gov.uk/assetRoot/04/01/90/79/04019079.pdf

13. DOH 2001b. *Good practice in consent implementation guide: consent to examination or treatment.* Available online:
    http://www.dh.gov.uk/assetRoot/04/01/90/61/04019061.pdf

14. DOH 2003. *Confidentiality: NHS Code of Practice.* Available online:
    http://www.dh.gov.uk/assetRoot/04/06/92/54/04069254.pdf

15. DOH 2005. *Records management: NHS code of practice consultation.* Available online:
    http://www.dh.gov.uk/Consultations/ClosedConsultations/
    ClosedConsultationsArticle/fs/en?CONTENT_ID=4119931&chk=D1y2nX

16. GMC 2002. *Making and using visual and audio recordings of patients.* Available online:
    http://www.gmc-uk.org/guidance/current/library/making_audiovisual.asp

17. GMC 1998. *Seeking patients' consent: the ethical considerations.* Available online:
    http://www.gmc-uk.org/guidance/current/library/consent.asp

18. GMC 2004a. *Confidentiality: protecting and providing information.* Available online:
    http://www.gmc-uk.org/guidance/current/library/confidentiality.asp
    GMC 2004b. *Confidentiality: protecting and providing information – Frequently Asked Questions.*
    Available online:
    http://www.gmc-uk.org/guidance/current/library/confidentiality_faq.asp

19. Institute of Medical Illustrators 1998. *A code of responsible practice – protocols for ethical conduct and legal compliance for medical illustrators.* IMI.

20. Institute of Medical Illustrators 2002. *Photography and video recordings of patients: confidentiality and consent, copyright and storage.* Model policy and procedure. Available online:
    http://www.imi.org.uk/imidocs/Model%20Consent.pdf

21. BMA 2004. *Taking and using visual and audio images of patients: Guidance from the medical ethics department.* Available online:
    http://www.bma.org.uk/ap.nsf/Content/AVrecordings

22. Royal College of Psychiatrists 1998. *Guidance for videotaping.* No longer available online.

23. Royal College of General Practitioners

24. Higher Education Academy, The, LTSN-01 FAQ information on AV materials and consent; FAQ 2004. No longer available online.

25. Creative Commons
http://creativecommons.org

26. HIPAA (Health Insurance Portability and Accountability Act 1996)
http://www.hipaa.org

27. Academy of Medical Sciences 2006: *Personal Data for Public Good: Using Health Information in Medical Research*. Available online:
http://www.acmedsci.ac.uk/images/project/Personal.pdf

Further reading

Addenbrooke's NHS Trust 2002. *Photography and video recordings of patients: confidentiality and consent, copyright and storage. Policy and Procedure.* Available online:
http://www.addenbrookes.org.uk/resources/pdf/photo/photo_procedure_180702.pdf

Bedford Hospitals NHS Trust 2005: *Visual and Audio Recording on Hospital Premises.* Contact details:
website http://www.bedfordhospital.org.uk/index.asp

Cardiff and Vale NHS Trust/Cardiff University 2005. *Policy for making and using illustrative clinical records.* Further information and contact details
http://www.cardiff.ac.uk/schoolsanddivisions/divisions/insrv/mediaresources/information/clinicalphotography.html

Corti L 1999. Text, sound and videotape: the future of qualitative data in the global network. *IASSIST Quarterly* 23:2, pp18-25. Available online:
http://iassistdata.org/publications/iq/iq23/iqvol232corti.pdf

Ellaway, R. 2004. *Modeling Virtual Patients and Virtual Cases.* MELD. Available online:
http://meld.medbiq.org/primers/virtual_patients_cases_ellaway.htm

Gloucestershire Hospitals NHS Foundation Trust 2005. *Photography and video recordings of patients: confidentiality and consent, copyright and storage* (draft). Contact details:
http://www.gloshospitals.org.uk/default.htm

Great Ormond Street Hospital NHS Trust. *Policy for making and using illustrative clinical records of patients.* Reproduced in full in appendix D (with kind permission of Jeremy Naylor, Director of Medical Illustration).

Hood C, Hope T, Dove P; 1998. Videos, photographs, and patient consent. *BMJ* 316:1009-1011
Available online:
http://bmj.bmjjournals.com/cgi/content/full/316/7136/1009

Information Commissioner's Office 2002. *Use and disclosure of health data* (p7). HMSO. Available online:
http://www.ico.gov.uk/upload/documents/library/data_protection/practical_application/health_data_-_use_and_disclosure001.pdf

Institute of Medical Illustrators website:
http://www.imi.org.uk/

Institute of Medical Illustrators 2004a. *Photography of non-accidental injuries*.
Available online:
http://www.imi.org.uk/guidelines/IMINatGuidelinesNAIMarch2006.pdf

Institute of Medical Illustrators 2004b. *Mole mapping photography*. Available
online:
http://www.imi.org.uk/guidelines/IMINatGuidelinesMoleMappingJuly2006.pdf

International Committee of Medical Journal Editors 1995. *Protection of patients'
rights to privacy*. BMJ 311:1272. Further information available online:
http://www.icmje.org/#privacy

Joint Committee for Postgraduate Training in General Practice 2002. *Guidelines
for videotaping of consultations*. Available online:
http://www.nosa.org.uk/information/video/cogped/code.htm

Norfolk and Norwich University Hospital NHS Trust 2004. *The management of
digital clinical images and video recordings*. Available online:
http://www.nnuh.nhs.uk/viewTrustDoc.asp?ID=108

Royal College of Radiologists 1998. *Making the best use of a department of clinical
radiology: Guidelines for doctors*. Fourth edition.

Smith R 1998. *Patients' consent for publication of information about them*. bmj.com
COPE (Committee on Publication Ethics) Report 1998. Available online:
http://bmj.bmjjournals.com/misc/cope/tex7.shtml

The Royal Liverpool Children's Inquiry Full Report 2001. Available online:
http://www.rlcinquiry.org.uk/download/index.htm

Tóth P 2005, Creative Humbug *INDICARE Monitor* vol. 2, no. 4, available online:
http://www.indicare.org/tiki-read_article.php?articleId=118

University Hospital Birmingham NHS Foundation Trust 2003. *Photographic and
video recording consent and confidentiality policy*. Available online:
http://www.uhb.nhs.uk/about/policies/policies/all_policies/20030505%20
Photographic%20%20Video%20Consent%20Policy.pdf

University of California- Los Angeles. *Consent for and authorization for release
of photographs, films, medical images, and other multimedia for educational
purposes*. Available from smcintyre@mednet.ucla.edu

Chapter 6

Digital Image Archiving: An Evidence-Based, Life-Cycle Approach to Management, Preservation and Access

Sheila Anderson
Director, Arts and Humanities Data Service

ai Suspension Bridge, by G Arnald
stitution of Civil Engineers (ICE).

Digital Image Archiving: An Evidence-Based, Life-Cycle Approach to Management, Preservation and Access

http://www.ahds.ac.uk/about/projects/archiving-studies/index.htm

Born-digital and digitised images form an important part of the digital collections that are central to the work of the scholarly community. The long-term availability of these digital assets, however, requires significant effort to ensure that they can survive changes of technology and can be accessed in the future.

Over the past few years, JISC has funded a series of feasibility studies that aim to assess the preservation risk and retention criteria for various types of digital content, and to help inform the development of future services and other initiatives in digital preservation. The Digital Images Archiving study forms part of this feasibility study programme and was funded to scope the preservation requirements of digital image files and to determine archiving methodologies and future research directions.

This chapter summarises a detailed and comprehensive study that represents an important step in advancing our understanding of many specific issues related to the long-term archiving and preservation of digital images. In the context of a life-cycle model for digital images, the author highlights issues around:

- how user requirements should affect preservation decisions and policies

- file formats and properties of digital images

- available and appropriate preservation methods

- organisational models and costs of preservation

The chapter also points out areas, such as the automated creation of preservation metadata, in which further work and research are required. This will help JISC to plan future work, leading to more in-depth understanding of the nature of digital images, and will contribute to the development of the necessary tools and infrastructure to support their long-term preservation.

Helen Hockx-Yu
PLANETS Project Manager, British Library and previously Programme Manager, JISC Development

Introduction

The growth in digital technologies has meant that a vast number of digital images, both raster and vector, is produced every year. The scholarly community is making particular use of this new content in research, teaching and practice, and digitisation of collections has allowed a radical shift in the manner in which libraries, cultural organisations and other content owners can deliver their collections, enabling them to provide round-the-clock online access to multiple users from anywhere in the world.

Management and preservation requirements for digital materials are fundamentally different from those for non-digital materials. Digital materials can be created using a wide range of technologies and formats, whether born digital or digital surrogates of existing non-digital materials. They can be described and documented in a variety of ways – or not at all. They are subject to both physical deterioration and technical obsolescence. More than one copy can be easily and simply created. Access may be provided through more than one point, and may be distributed. All these factors will impinge upon the approach taken to their management and long-term preservation.

These differences present the curators of digital materials with some fundamental challenges. The way in which materials are created, particularly the technologies used, will determine how conducive to long-term preservation the materials are, and will present varied challenges to curators charged with the subsequent management and preservation of the materials. Curators will need adequate metadata about the resource if they are to successfully manage and preserve the materials, and make them accessible. Multiple copies may also imply multiple versions – the digital-resource curator must somehow ensure the integrity and authenticity of the resource. He/she must be aware of changing technologies and the fragility of media and take these into consideration from an early stage in the ingest process.

Access and preservation of digital content are, of course, closely linked. Jones and Beagrie define digital preservation as: '...the series of managed activities necessary to ensure continued access to digital materials for as long as necessary. Digital preservation...refers to all the actions required to maintain access to digital materials beyond the limits of media failure or technological change'[1].

All this suggests that digital curation and preservation require a more pro-active approach beginning at an earlier stage in the material's life cycle than would traditionally be the case with non-digital materials. Within the digital preservation community, the concept of the life-cycle (or continuum, as it is sometimes called) management of digital resources has emerged to describe and document the active management processes that need to take place, and the key decision-making and intervention points along the continuum. The life-cycle concept has been incorporated into the Open Archival Information System (OAIS) reference model, now adopted as an ISO standard for digital preservation[2]. The OAIS model is proving a strong foundation for the development of digital archiving projects and services, and is increasingly being implemented by digital libraries, archives and data services.

However, despite these developments, the difficulty for those undertaking preservation or with responsibility for providing access in the long term to digital resources is the lack of practical advice, and of robust tools and mature techniques for digital preservation. A number of digital-preservation strategies have been proposed, but there is no definitive approach to the problem of maintaining digital content across multiple generations of technology. Unfortunately, information on the likely costs, possible limitations and long-term sustainability of different strategies is far from complete – partly, it must be said, for the very valid reason that no one has yet had the time to gain the experience needed to answer these questions.

The work undertaken for the Digital Images Archiving Study set out to overcome some of these limitations, with the dual aim of providing a firm foundation which JISC could use in its future decision-making, and acting as a valuable resource for those creating, managing, curating, providing access to and preserving digital images.

Scope of the study

The definition of a digital image we used in our study is as follows:

> 'Digital (still) images are non-moving representations of visual information.'

That is, still images that convey their meaning in visual terms, e.g. photographs, posters, diagrams, drawings. The study considers both the familiar raster image and the perhaps less well-known vector image. The former includes the products of digital photography and scanning with file formats such as TIFF and JPEG. Less consideration seems to have given to vector images in the literature, but a large volume of vector digital content is created, much of it born digital, including maps, drawings and the almost ubiquitous PDF file.

Both raster and vector images can be said to be geometric or spatial, but any similarities end there. Raster (or bit-mapped) images are grid-based, with information being held about each point or pixel within the grid, whereas vector images have information about any number X, Y, Z spatially defined coordinates and are made up of scalable objects – lines, curves and shapes – defined in mathematical terms, often with typographic insertions.

Initially, we sought to embed the work of our study within current research. However, we found a (somewhat surprising) distinct lack of research dedicated to the preservation of digital images, and a consequent lack of practical advice, robust tools and mature techniques for the digital preservation of images. What research there has been to date has tended to be theoretically based, and although test-bed projects have begun to emerge, overall most research tends to be general in nature rather than, say, investigating TIFF as an image-preservation format.

Although work specific to digital-image preservation is rare, there are two or three areas in particular where useful practical work is taking place. For example, the programme to develop a decision support framework for the preservation of a range of content types currently underway at the Library of Congress is providing useful, focused research and practical guidance[3]. Further work of this kind to identify the complexities, risk factors and risk assessment processes would be of enormous value to the preservation community, and would facilitate informed decision-making at all stages of the digital life cycle. In the UK, the Arts and Humanities Data Service (AHDS)[4] is grappling with the practicalities of preserving both raster and vector images, and has written guides to good practice, and preservation handbooks for both types of image. These are publicly available through the AHDS website. Similarly the Technical Advisory Service for Images (TASI)[5] provides useful advice for those creating digital images that includes a discussion of preservation issues on its website.

Our study focused on addressing a number of practical issues related to the preservation of images. First among these is the nature of digital images themselves – their content, format, size, metadata requirements – and potential preservation methods to ensure long-term access and use. We also addressed user-community requirements, both for those creating digital images and for subsequent users. These issues are set within the concept of the life cycle of the digital image, and the nature of digital repositories as outlined in the OAIS model and the work on trusted digital repositories[6].

Life-Cycle Model for digital images

Discussion of digital repositories, and their role in curating and preserving digital content, centres around several activities. The OAIS model summarises these as:

- Ingest
- Archival storage
- Access
- Data management
- Administration
- Preservation planning

There are a couple of assumptions underlying these activities. First, that they take place as a life-cycle management of digital content, and second, that such repositories serve a designated community – that is, the community of stakeholders who have an interest in the content of the repository. Our study used these as the starting point in its thinking about the requirements for preserving and curating digital images.

Working to that brief, the research produced a simple schematic model that identifies the key events that take place during the life cycle, the activities that are likely to take place at those event points, and the policies and processes that underpin those activities and events. The model emphasises that the process of curating and preserving digital images starts at the point of creation, working with the creators wherever possible, and continues with the curators, taking account of the designated community in the decisions it makes. It is presented as a managed process in which actions are taken at identified points to ensure the future accessibility and usability of the image.

At each key event a range of actions is, or should, be taken that will affect the future of the digital images. Many of these actions will affect the longer-term survival of the images and will determine whether they are merely a collection of bits, or something that remains fit for purpose over time and changing requirements. The key concept is the construction of 'a managed environment' that facilitates the ongoing decision-making and actions required to sustain accessibility and usability and to preserve digital objects themselves.

Figure 6.1
The Life-Cycle Model for digital images.

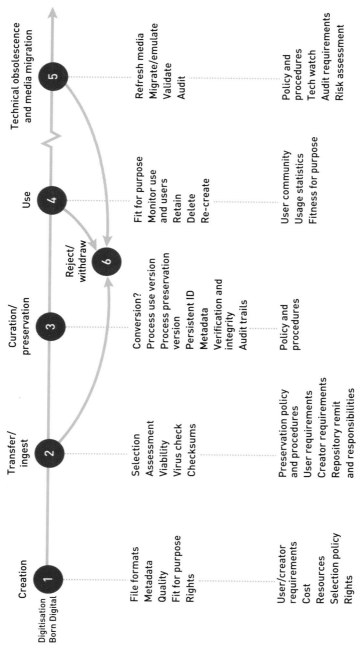

The model identifies the key events that take place, the activities that should take place at those events, and the policies and processes that underpin them. Thus the top layer conveys the idea that this is part of a continuum where key action points are identified; the second layer outlines the actions and decisions that are likely to be made at this time; and the third identifies the requirements, policies and processes on which these decisions are likely to be based.

User requirements

It is now widely accepted that the development of a digital system, like any non-digital system, should be led by an understanding of the needs of those people who will use it. The Digital Images Preservation Study gives great weight to what we have termed end-users, but it also includes within this remit those who are engaged with digitising or creating born-digital images – the so-called start-users. The study argues that consideration must be given in the digital image preservation process to the users of those images, and that the process must also engage with the creators of image collections wherever possible. Identifying the designated community and understanding its ongoing and possibly changing needs is a key factor in managing digital images, and their subsequent dissemination.

Our research found that user concerns are dominated by worries, some founded and some speculative, relating to – first and foremost – access and the metadata required to facilitate access. This is followed closely by concern with the difficult issue of copyright/IPR, and with the more transient nature of digital image formats, issues of quality and of changes in technology. We would therefore argue that it is not just the technology and systems that must be considered, but also the connection between *technological facility* and *human factors*. Just as the different image formats develop, change or migrate into emerging formats, so a system must adapt and grow in response to issues relating to change of use, copyright, wider accessibility and even metadata, within the communities that the system is designed to serve.

The concept of the life-cycle model developed for the report on our study identifies that preservation starts with the data-creation process and must include regular monitoring and response to user needs and requirements if the right preservation decisions are to be made. For example, it is pointless for an image repository to migrate its content to one format, when the community doesn't use that format or have access to software that accepts it. Similarly, an archive might concentrate on creating technical metadata that fits its preservation needs, but if it is not accompanied by metadata that enables discovery and use, then it is questionable whether the repository is fulfilling its remit.

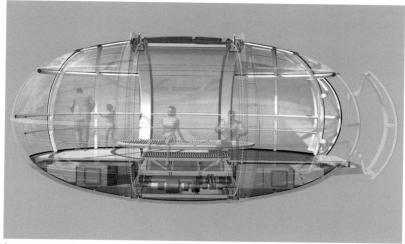

Cutaway drawing of a passenger capsule – British Airways London Eye
Image by Nic Bailey, © Marks Barfield', via the Institution of Civil Engineers (ICE) Virtual Library.

Furthermore, preservation decisions must be based on the content and nature of the image, and different preservation decisions and actions may be taken depending on these factors. For example, if the content of an image is unique (an original artwork for example, or a set of architectural drawings), then the approach to preservation may well be different to something that is more common or has less value in terms of use (although assessing value is very difficult). Similarly, the nature of the image will affect preservation approaches and actions. For example, if precise colour depth and accuracy are not essential characteristics (as may be the case with many vector graphics), then the preservation approach is likely to reflect this. The concept of fitness for purpose is crucial to these ideas and should be factored into the preservation life-cycle approach. Fit for purpose means that what is provided meets the needs of the designated community as far as that is possible. In other words, a preservation approach is fit for purpose if it meets the reasonable expectations of the designated community it serves.

There seems to be a general assumption that we must preserve all digital content and every digital image that has been created. The concept of fitness for purpose brings that idea into question. What is fit for purpose now may not remain so in the future. The need for different types of content may change over time and, if past experience is anything to go by, standards of digitisation and image capture will continue to improve well beyond what is acceptable now. Such changes may well make a particular digital image obsolete in terms of quality and/or functionality, even though it can still be rendered and used in the technological sense.

Selection of images for preservation, and their subsequent retention, require more attention than seems to have been given to them thus far. We recommend that JISC should support the investigation of selection and retention issues, with the idea of fitness for purpose in mind. This should include assessing where the costs of digitising images lie. It may be that the most costly part is the creation of metadata rather than the capture of the digital image. In that case, JISC might recommend or require properly managed preservation of the metadata and surrounding information, alongside a programme to re-digitise the image content at such time as the nature of the object no longer meets the needs of the user communities.

However, if the cost of digitising the object is high, and the image content is born digital, or digitised from a fragile or very rare and hard to access analogue, then a different approach is necessary: the image must be created to the best achievable standards and properly preserved into the future, alongside the metadata. We argue in the full report that a 'one-size-fits-all' approach to preservation is short sighted and recommend further investigation of how user requirements and fitness for purpose might be factored into preservation decisions and actions. We suggest the need for a range of different approaches that reflect the requirements of the future community of users, as well as the more prosaic technological requirements.

To achieve appropriate (and hence cost-effective) selection, retention and preservation regimes, we need to know and understand more about how and why users are both creating and using digital images of all kinds, and it behoves us all to capture and analyse usage data in as much depth as possible to feed back into our understanding and practice.

Properties and file formats

As noted earlier, access to and preservation of digital content are closely linked. The conversion of binary data into meaningful information relies on a complex chain of hardware, software and formats, all of which are subject to ongoing technological change. Consequently, providing long-term access to digital content inevitably involves the challenges of digital preservation. Content in a digital repository must be protected from the problems of data corruption and technological obsolescence, and the authenticity of the content must be ensured in some way. However, it must also be fit for purpose over time. This means that attention must be paid to establishing the significant properties and addressing the issue of file formats. To enable decision-making about preservation we use the following three-tiered representation:

1. Preservation of the bit stream (basic sequences of binary digits) that ultimately represent the information stored in any digital resource

2. Preservation of the *information content* (images, sounds, moving images etc.) stored as bits and defined by a logical data model, embodied in a file or media format

3. Preservation of the *experience* (speed, layout, display device, input-device characteristics etc.) of interacting with the information content

All three still present challenges for digital preservation, although the first is perhaps easier than the second and third.

File (or data) formats define the rules used by application software to convert bits (the fundamental unit of digital data) into meaningful information that can be viewed and manipulated by a user. Most application-software developers produce file-format documentation for the formats they design and develop. Not all of them make this documentation available and, even if they do, it is not always accurate.

Based on the availability and stability of the format specification, file formats can be classified as proprietary, open or standard formats. *Proprietary file formats* are not made public and are developed and maintained by software producers.

Larger software producers may sometimes publish their format specifications as Publicly Available Specifications (PAS), or several firms may join together in a consortium to define interface standards so that they can develop mutually compatible products. These are called *open or public file formats*.

Some file formats are developed to become international standards (*standard file formats*) that are then public and fixed or stable until the next release of the standard.

It is not unusual for software companies to produce their own modified, proprietary versions of standard file formats – these will be based on standards, but will have extensions that are proprietary and generally not public (e.g. Microsoft's version of XML). Many proprietary formats are, nevertheless, widely used and provide extensive compatibility with application software – these formats are often classified as *de facto* standards.

Successful long-term preservation of a digital file depends on the openness, level of standardisation and compatibility with other software products of the file format. Without a format specification the vital rendering tools that enable the use of digital files over a longer time cannot be developed. Reverse engineering of software or the digital objects themselves can provide some answers, although legal constraints may well prevent this kind of action. Even where reverse engineering is possible, without any file-format documentation the process is likely to be too laborious and expensive.

The preservation risks associated with file formats are mostly related to loss of data and cost. Both migration and emulation – the two best digital-preservation strategies currently in use – rely on file-format specification being known and accurate. If it is not, then preservation actions risk introducing distortion, loss of quality or data, or not being able to render the file usable at all. The risk management of file formats for preservation has to take account of all these considerations.

Vector images

We have identified significant challenges for the preservation of vector images. The file formats and software applications used to create such images are numerous, are frequently proprietary, and many generate binary files which can be problematic for longer-term preservation. Fortunately, many – but not all – allow for export as structured ASCII text, and that is generally accepted as being the most stable of formats. However, an ASCII export is not enough in itself. Its meaning has to be openly documented

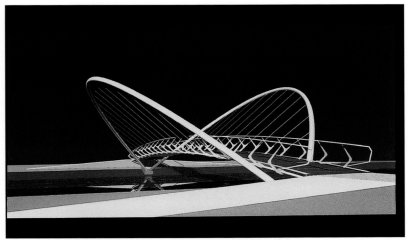

Bedford footbridge, from the talk *Bridging Art & Science* by Chris Wilkinson
© Hayes Davidson (Computer rendering), via Pidgeon Digital.

in order that the data can be reconstructed for use in another software application. This can be expensive and time-consuming, as it usually involves a great deal of human effort to capture the correct information. It may also place a significant burden on subsequent users, as a relatively high level of expertise is likely to be required to manipulate and import the data. Moreover, the risk over the longer term of degradation and loss of functionality associated with this approach is unknown. Work to assess these risks and to develop alternative approaches is urgently required.

Whist such work would make significant strides towards ensuring the long-term preservation of much vector data, there is also a need for work to maintain information on the most suitable software to render these data in the future. The JISC community therefore needs to collaborate to ensure the creation of a registry of common file formats that is updated regularly with comments on new and emerging formats and their suitability for use. This should go beyond the usual format registry that advises on suitable preservation formats and provides technical details, to include information useful to users when making decisions about which formats and software to use. There is a requirement with many of these formats to capture additional information that may not necessarily appear in the structured metadata. For example, CAD (Computer-Aided Design) files require fairly detailed information about the methodology and tools used to capture or create the image. If this additional information is not recorded, it can affect the long-term understandability of the data and thus degrade the value of the image.

We advise that further research and development in the area of the preservation of vector-image data is made a priority for future action to deal with the issues identified here, which are described in more detail in the full report of our study.

Raster images

The situation with raster images is less complex. TIFF[7] is widely regarded as a de-facto preservation standard and the emergence of JPEG2000[8] may well prove to be an acceptable standard for preservation. However, the lack of research to test these assumptions is worrying and it is recommended that research into the long-term suitability of both TIFF and JPEG2000 be commissioned. In particular there is a need to undertake further work to investigate the variability of TIFF and the consequences of not including additional functionality that is available in some revisions. Similarly PNG[9] may offer potential, but as yet has little industry support and has the same problem of additional functionality as TIFF. DNG[10] has been developed by Adobe to work with RAW[11] files that arise primarily from digital cameras. This may also become a standard archive format.

The difficulty facing the preservation community is to stay up to date with these new and emerging formats, and to properly understand what their potential is and what the main problems are with relying on any of them as preservation formats. Finding clear and concise advice is problematic and the community needs to develop 'information nodes' where this information can be easily located and understood. The need for a comprehensive 'tech watch' to identify new formats, to research their usefulness for preservation and to warn of the problems and risks associated with each, is urgent. Difficult as this might be, as far as possible it should also include a dialogue with industry in order, at best, to influence developments in the area and, at worst, at least to understand what industry is doing and why.

In addition, it would be most useful to define a common set of significant properties for both raster and vector images; that is, those characteristics of the image that must be preserved over time. The defining of these properties should be undertaken in collaboration with the community of users, to ensure that their needs are taken into account.

Preservation methods

Digital image data in whichever format remains useful only for as long as it can be correctly *rendered* (displayed, played back, interacted with) into meaningful content such as text, images and video clips. The process of rendering is performed by a complex mix of hardware and software, which is subject to rapid obsolescence. As a rule of thumb, it is reasonable to predict that current hardware and software will be able to correctly render a file for around ten years after its creation. By the end of this period, repositories need to have adopted a more active preservation strategy than simply preserving the bit stream of the file if they are to maintain access to information content held in the file. Either old data must be altered to operate in a new technical environment (through migration and format standardisation) or the new environment must be modified so that it can render the old data (through emulation and virtual computers). Within these two broad approaches there are many different techniques, a number of which are set out in Figure 6.2.

The relative merits of technology preservation, migration, emulation, migration on request and the universal virtual computer (UVC) summarised here, are discussed in detail in our report. Format migration and format standardisation appear to be the most common approaches for both vector and raster images, although significant problems arise when dealing with vector image files.

Figure 6.2
Digital Preservation Strategies (based on Thibodeau, 2002)[12]

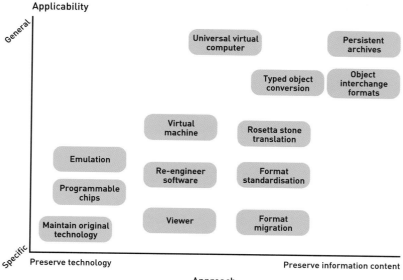

Emulation, migration on request and UVC all pose significant problems and require the injection of major programmes (and funds) to create the necessary migration and rendering tools and decoders. At the present time it seems unlikely that these methods will be viable for repositories; unless and until the tools exist to undertake these processes they are likely to remain only in test-bed environments rather than as working methods in actual repositories. The difficulty with emulation, migration on request and UVC approaches is the technical effort required to create the tasks to emulate or migrate on request. Whilst in theory all these approaches have merit, and look very attractive in some cases, the fundamental problem arises that unless there is a coordinated effort to create the tools (and to create and sustain them as open source, so that all can use them), to archive the tools and to make them widely and freely available through tools registries, it is difficult to see how they can be fully relied upon and implemented within working repositories.

However, it would be wrong to deny the potential of these methods, and the community needs to keep a watching brief on developments in this area; should suitable tools emerge from the research and development that is currently underway, then developmental implementation in working repositories is a distinct possibility. For the time being, however, it seems that format migration along with format standardisation is the most reliable approach, and should be implemented.

In terms of preservation practice, the report recommends that curators archive a copy of the original file in the event that emulation or other techniques become viable in the future. Retention of source bitstreams is a necessary component of any preservation approach, to safeguard against migration errors and choices of preservation formats that might prove to be incorrect over time. It is also important to bear in mind that preservation formats are not necessarily distribution/delivery formats (although dissemination/delivery versions of digital images may be in the same file format as the preservation copies), and very careful consideration needs to be given to selecting the 'master copy' for preservation.

Some other points need to be made:

- There is no single best way to preserve any digital resource
- Decisions about preservation approaches depend on resources available, current and future use of the resources, and the cultural/historical/ social/legal significance of the resources
- Decisions made about the recommended preservation formats for individual resources can change over time

Again, we would emphasise that, at the present time, preservation is best regarded as a series of managed actions, all of which should be properly documented. By doing this, curators may be able to retrace their steps to better understand the process.

Raster images

At the present time the most reliable form of preservation for raster images is the format migration approach. We recommend this as the default, but archives and repositories are also strongly recommended to keep copies of images in their original format as created or deposited. This would ensure that, should other preservation methods such as emulation or UVC became viable options in the future, these can be adapted as necessary.

The use of uncompressed TIFF version 6 is the best strategy at the current time, but a watching brief should be maintained on JPEG2000 as an emerging preservation format. Should, as seems likely, industry support for JPEG2000 grow, then this may well sit alongside TIFF as the format of choice. A similar watching brief should be kept on PNG and DNG.

Vector images

The situation with regard to vector files is much more complicated, primarily due to the large number of vector-image software applications in use, and the fact that many of these use proprietary binary formats. These difficulties are compounded by the lack of non-proprietary open formats. Whilst support for the Open Geospatial Consortium (OGC)[13] data formats is growing, it is not yet widespread. There is clearly a need for more cooperation and sharing of knowledge and expertise in this area, and a focus for promoting more widespread uptake and use across the industry.

Recommending a suitable preservation format is much more difficult for vector images and the approach will differ according to the purpose of the original data. The approaches listed in the report of our study were done on the basis that they be regarded as interim suggestions only, and that they should not be relied upon for preservation of such files in excess of ten years. The lowest-common-denominator approach would be to export the data as structured ASCII text with the creation of additional documentation that describes the meaning of the ASCII text structure and how to recompose it for use. There is an added complication in that this is not a particularly user-friendly approach and does not encourage re-use of the materials. It is also fairly labour-intensive and hence adds to the costs. Unfortunately it is difficult at this stage to recommend any other approach, and so further research is needed in this area as a matter of priority.

Metadata

There are three types of metadata that must be considered in the preservation of digital images. These are technical metadata, management (administrative) metadata and discovery/use metadata. Technical metadata is necessary to describe the physical attributes of digital objects and is particularly important for preservation and rendering. Management metadata is essential to ensure that authenticity, rights, ownership and provenance are properly addressed. Discovery and use metadata is essential to ensure future use of digital objects – being able to locate, access and use digital content in the long term is arguably the *raison d'être* of preservation.

For raster images a range of metadata standards exists that might be used to capture and structure metadata, starting with basic Dublin Core[14] for discovery and use, through more comprehensive standards such as VRA Core 3.0,[15] PREMIS[16], and NISO Z39.87[17]. Each has its strengths and weaknesses. For example VRA Core is very well suited to describing digital representations, as it also provides a facility to describe the original work and any surrogate analogue such as a slide. However, it does not include a comprehensive set of technical metadata elements, and cannot therefore meet the requirements for preservation. Z39.87 provides a comprehensive metadata set, but it may prove too comprehensive to enable wide take-up. The burden placed upon creators and curators of digital images to create metadata to this standard may be too high, as may the costs involved.

We therefore suggest a somewhat pragmatic approach and recommend a generic standard that maps across these more comprehensive standards. A convergence between the generic elements of PREMIS and the mostly mandatory file-information section of Z39.87 is therefore proposed. We also recommend the use of METS[18] as a flexible wrapper within which the different element sets could be combined and preserved.

Yet again, vector image formats present more of a problem. There are a number of emerging standards at different levels of development and acceptance for CAD, GIS, VRML[19] and SVG[20], and at this time it is not possible to make concrete recommendations. There is some urgency then to undertake work to identify the common properties applicable to most (if not all) vector formats, and to work with the standards community to achieve this aim.

Creating metadata is currently somewhat time-consuming, and to create the range and quality required for the ever-increasing volume of digital images is likely to prove extremely difficult with current levels of funding. There has been some useful early work to create tools to automatically extract or modify metadata, and it would be welcome if effort could be made to create or modify these tools (e.g. JHOVE, NLNZ Metadata Extractor Tool) so that they generate standardised and compatible metadata compliant with PREMIS and key format-specific schemas, such as Z39.87/MIX. Such tools should adopt elements from established namespaces and avoid the use of application-specific schemas.

Work could also usefully be performed to improve the tools used for metadata extraction to simplify the batch-processing of a large number of files in a collection and generating distinct XML records for each object. To maintain the validity of the original collection, XML records should be output to a directory structure that mirrors the original. Related to this, further work might usefully be undertaken to extend the range of common file formats recognized by metadata extraction tools, alongside the development of scenarios and workflows for integrating the manual and automatic production of metadata for digital still images.

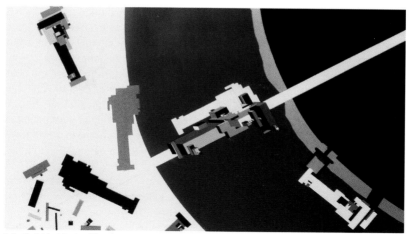

Zaha Hadid Architectural Drawing
© Zaha Hadid, via Pidgeon Digital.

For discovery and access purposes, we are starting to see the development and use of techniques such as text mining and automated extraction of key words using pattern-recognition software. However, as yet, most of the tools in these new areas are quite difficult to use for the layperson. It may prove worthwhile for the curatorial community to work alongside the software engineers and developers to improve the interfaces and functionality of these tools, and to test them in working repositories. Similarly, the emergence of 'folksonomies' (where communities add their own metadata until a critical mass builds up around a resource) points to another technique worth pursuing in a test-bed situation. The community needs to work together to find solutions to the problem of creating comprehensive metadata for an ever-expanding volume of digital content.

Organisation models and costs

There is a range of organisational models that might be suitable for ensuring the preservation of digital images of all kinds, from single-site models through to a number of different formations of disaggregation. These include:

- Single-institution image repositories

- Image repository with specialist support for preservation

- Image repository with outsourced preservation services

- Outsourced image repository services

Two key factors need to be considered if both fitness for purpose and the concept of the managed environment are to be addressed. These are that by and large images arise from and are used by subject specialists – visual arts practitioners, architecture students, geographers and so on. Users of image archives will also come with a subject orientation, and thus subject requirements must be considered for preservation. In addition, there are technical characteristics, many of which are outlined in the full report, that define digital images, and these must also be considered when preserving them. We therefore recommend the development of some form of disaggregated model that can encompass both these needs .

The full report of our study discusses the likely costs associated with the preservation of digital images. It provides a brief overview of the methods for assessing costs but is unable to give figures, largely because we do not yet have the practical experience to do so. However, there is an increasing number of studies and reports on assessing costs, and some repositories have identified the costs of establishing and running a repository. It would be useful if the community had access to these studies and reports in a single place, alongside a commentary on the work undertaken so far. This would enable image repositories at least to define their methodology for assessing likely costs and assist in the development of appropriate business plans that would ensure financial stability and sustainability – essential if a repository is to conform to trusted digital-repository requirements.

Conclusions

Our research demonstrates that there is still work to be done before we can rest assured that we are adequately preserving digital images. Clearly, the major problem lies with vector images, where urgent research and development are required and where the community needs to come together to investigate and find solutions for the multitude of problems that exist in this area. However, we should not lose sight of the extent to which we still do not know and understand the consequences of our actions with raster images. Whilst we have a greater understanding and share more commonalities across the raster image-using community, there are still considerable gaps in our knowledge that need to be filled.

Several practical community activities could take place to increase our knowledge and understanding. In a similar fashion to standards development communities, we might organise working groups to identify sets of significant properties for both raster and vector graphics. These groups could decide what properties really matter and for whom, which in turn would assist repository managers to focus their selection and retention policies on acquiring and preserving those formats which best meet the needs of their designated communities. Alongside this, we might usefully undertake work to test how different formats manage and preserve these characteristics, and to provide format registries in the form of look-up tables that provide this information with user-friendly interfaces.

This work also has the potential to translate into advice for those creating digital images, to inform preservation actions and methods, and accessibility and dissemination methods.

We also need to undertake more work on the automation of metadata creation and extraction. However, this should be tied into the user community. What will they trust? How do they use the metadata, and what is essential for their purposes? What is essential for curation? If repositories are able to automate all metadata creation, but it is not what the community wants or needs, then we are all wasting our time.

Perhaps the final additional point to be made is that we need to work from a properly formed evidence base, regardless of the task in hand. We need more evidence of how people are using these images, how they find them and how they manipulate them. We need more evidence of the consequences of the technical decisions that we make and the formats in which we choose to store our images. We need to continue to share expertise and knowledge so that we build up a comprehensive knowledge and evidence base for the work that we do, and so that we can place as much confidence in digital-image repositories as we do in the galleries, libraries and archives that we trust to curate and preserve our non-digital heritage.

References

1. Jones, M and Beagrie, N, 2002. *Preservation Management of Digital Materials: a Handbook*. British Library, London.

2. ISO 14721:2003. Space data and information transfer systems – Open archival information system – Reference model. Available online: http://www.iso.org/iso/en/CatalogueDetailPage.CatalogueDetail?CSNUMBER =24683&ICS1=49&ICS2=140&ICS3

3. Library of Congress research and practical guidance available online: http://www.digitalpreservation.gov/formats/intro/intro.shtml.

4. AHDS (Arts and Humanities Data Service) http://www.ahds.ac.uk

5. TASI (Technical Advisory Service for Images)
   http://www.tasi.ac.uk

6. A trusted digital repository is one whose mission is to provide reliable, long-term access to managed resources now and in the future. Further information on the work in the area of trusted digital repositories carried out by RLG and OCLC, and subsequently by RLG and NARA can be found at: http://www.rlg.org/;
   the attributes of a Trusted Digital Repository are set out in our full report, p.93-94.

7. Tagged Image File Format. The Adobe TIFF resources page is available online: http://partners.adobe.com/public/developer/tiff/index.html
   The specification TIFF Revision 6.0, Final – June 3, 1992 is available online: http://partners.adobe.com/public/developer/en/tiff/TIFF6.pdf

8. JPEG2000 (The Joint Photographic Experts Group):
   http://www.jpeg.org/jpeg2000/

9. PNG (The Portable Network Graphics):
   http://www.libpng.org/pub/png/

10. DNG (Digital Negative):
    http://www.adobe.com/products/dng/

11. OpenRAW:
    http://www.openraw.org/

12. Thibodeau, K., 2002. 'Overview of Technological Approaches to Digital Preservation and Challenges in Coming Years', *Proceedings of The State of Digital Preservation: An International Perspective*. Council on Library and Information Resources, Washington, D.C.

13. OGC (Open Geospatial Consortium)
    http://www.opengeospatial.org/

14. Dublin Core Metadata Initiative
    http://dublincore.org/

15. Visual Resources Association VRA Core Categories, Version 3.0
    http://www.vraweb.org/projects/vracore3/index.html

16. PREMIS (Preservation Metadata: Implementation Strategies)
    http://www.loc.gov/standards/premis/

17. NISO Z39.87 Data Dictionary – Technical Metadata for Digital Still Images. Released as a Draft Standard for Trial Use, June 1, 2002 – December 31, 2003. http://www.niso.org/standards/resources/Z39_87_trial_use.pdf
    At the time of writing it is in the comment period of the review process (1 May 2006 – 15 June 2006).

18. METS – Metadata Encoding & Transmission Standard:
    http://www.loc.gov/standards/mets/

19. Virtual Reality Modeling Language (VRML). VRML 97 and Related Specifications
    http://www.web3d.org/x3d/specifications/vrml/

20. Scalable Vector Graphics (SVG)
    http://www.w3.org/Graphics/SVG/

Chapter 7

Next Steps to Realise the Vision

Leona Carpenter, Lorraine Estelle, Catherine Grout and Rachel Bruce, with Stuart Dempster, Helen Hockx-yu, Neil Jacobs, Balviar Notay, Amber Thomas, Philip Vaughan

on Slope of Hadley Delta

A life-cycle approach for image collections

Four clusters of common themes were identified as arising from the Images Working Group (IWG) digital image collection vision and the work reported in the preceding chapters. First, we need to know more about the creators of digital images, the users of digital images and the uses that are made of digital images. While *the* Digital Picture, CLIC and CHERRI studies made progress in this area, they also made clear that there is much still to be done.

Second, we must address trust, fear of risk and management of risk, especially in relation to copyright and intellectual property rights (IPR), to facilitate the use of digital images in further and higher education. The conflicts and complexities involved in copyright and IPR for digital images are seen as much more challenging than for text – for reasons summarised in chapter 2. Third, issues should be addressed relating to resource discovery, metadata and the need for tools and guidance to support the management and use of digital images. While text-based resources by their nature carry the fallback option of full-text searching, content-based image retrieval as an alternative to metadata searching within and across image collections is still at an experimental stage of development.

The entrance to Newgrange viewed face-on from the SE
© Archaeology data Archive, via The Archaeology Image Bank at the Archaeology Data Service.

Fourth, the challenges associated with the variety, complexity and speed of change in the area of digital images for education and research should also be addressed; and it was recognised that there is a consequent need for further research. Change at a technical level is seen in the evolution of digital-image formats and the emergence of new formats in response not only to usage and quality drivers, but also to legal challenges regarding the control and relative openness of format standards. And *the* Digital Picture initiative demonstrated that things also move on quickly at the level of practice. At the start of the study people were talking about floppy discs and were concerned about the demise of the 35mm slide, but by the end they had moved to networked environments and digital images rather than slides for creating and holding, as well as using, images.

The best way to address these issues is in the context of a life-cycle approach for image collections. The stages in the image-collection life cycle are shown in Figure 7.1, below.

Figure 7.1
A life-cycle approach for image collections.

It is important to note that these stages are not isolated from one another, and that within this high-level life cycle, more detailed life cycles and work flows are envisioned for particular areas. For example, a preservation life cycle as set out in chapter 6 includes activities that take place at the time of image creation.

Strategic aspects of a pragmatic life-cycle approach must take account of the need to license as well as digitise or create digital images; issues relating to portals and interoperability; and the imperative to leverage community assets. While some areas requiring action are most relevant to one specific stage of the life cycle, others cut across all or most stages, from creation to preservation.

The way ahead across the life cycle

Copyright and IPR issues arose in every study, and guidance in these areas is required to support the use and management of digital images, including:

- Are we clear enough about what constitutes 'educational use' in terms of copyright?

- Once a digital image has been discovered, how can I (as a student, researcher or lecturer) tell what I am allowed to do with it?

- If I'm allowed to do what I want to do, what will it cost?

These issues must be addressed, as must issues of ensuring authenticity and identifying provenance, consent for the creation of images and ethical considerations. IPR and ethical issues also arise in relation to making preservation copies of many classes of images, including especially – but not confined to – clinical recordings. When it comes to sharing images beyond institutional boundaries, institutions fear litigation and so are reluctant to take what they perceive as significant risks, related to copyright and IPR, which are involved in sharing.

Management of risk

The studies found that academics feel they do not know:

- who owns the images they use;

- what they have a right to do with the images;

- what their risks are in relation to the use and sharing of images.

In general, academics do not like the idea of transferring risk to their institutions by agreeing that their institutions 'own' the images they have created or accumulated – if only because it may well turn out that the institutions are even more averse to IPR risks than individual academics are, resulting in the desired increased availability of images not after all being realised. For digital images, this would appear to undercut the solution suggested in the Jorum[1] context, that institutions should take ownership of learning objects and warrant their level of share-ability.

Thus, there is a clear need for guidance in this area. The JISC-funded Technical Advisory Service for Images (TASI)[2] provides extensive guidance for staff using images for teaching and research, as well as for those building and managing digital image collections. TASI has recently made available updated and new guidance, some in response to the findings reported here, in the area of copyright and the responsibilities of the creators and users of images. In collaboration with consultant Naomi Korn, TASI has created in-depth advisory documents on copyright and digital images, roles and responsibilities for staff involved in building digital image collections, and for those using images for teaching and research. In addition, TASI has set out responses to frequently asked questions about copyright, based on questions that have been asked of the TASI Helpdesk, a service that responds to individual enquiries submitted via email. Thus, the Frequently Asked Questions document is based on situations that actually arise in UK further and higher education.

While there may be widespread awareness of the availability of TASI advice among most creators of image collections, activities are required to increase awareness of this vital service among users.

Guidance and a licence framework for clinical images

In addition to the copyright issues, for the use of clinical recordings – including both social-work and medical images – so important for education, and particularly for health-care education, there are issues of consent for both creation and use. In addition, there are the complications of proving and ensuring authenticity and provenance in relation to copyright, consent and ethical issues. There is a tension between the risks and benefits of making material available, and the risks and benefits of *not* making it available.

Current thinking, remembering that the CHERRI study represents a snapshot of a moment in the process of dealing with these issues, is that we require a common licensing framework: a 'clinical commons' that protects both patients and practitioners. Although any adopted model may or may not in the end be based on Creative Commons licences, the Creative Commons process and interface elements provide a useful starting point.

Another part of the solution is to provide practitioner guidance that includes exemplars and case studies. There is a substantial body of well-documented principles, but a lack of guidance on how to apply them. Two of the issues that must be taken into account in developing guidance are the need to accommodate the most disadvantaged user, and the necessity of showing verifiably that due diligence has been taken.

Hackney Empire
© East London Theatre Archive.

But whose responsibility is it to produce a licence framework and guidance, which must take account of policy in both the clinical and the educational sectors? To complicate matters, there are jurisdictional issues. Even within the UK, devolution is leading to greater differences than before between the legal frameworks in England, Scotland and Wales. The final report from the CHERRI study has been well received. The author, Rachel Ellaway, is continuing to pursue buy-in from a range of stakeholders through, for example, presenting the report to the Caldicott Guardians (senior staff in the NHS and social services appointed to protect patient information). These ongoing efforts are being supported by a small group of interested people, including representatives from the Higher Education Academy[3] and the NHS-HE Forum, and JISC has made available a small budget for travel costs involved in this work.

Licensing image collections from commercial providers

In further and higher education, users want a wide diversity of digital images for use in teaching and learning. No one collection can provide the range of images required. The educational community will use images from the many freely available collections that may be accessed on the Internet; bigfoto. com[4] and AICT[5] are just two examples of collections that provide images freely for educational purposes. However, many of the images required in education are not and are unlikely to be freely available and it will always be necessary to license images for educational purposes.

Unfortunately the licence agreements provided by commercial image owners are often geared to the commercial world and do not provide for the flexibility of use required in education. Some of the terms and conditions provided by commercial owners of digital images indeed present a barrier to use for the educational community. The recent report of the Gowers Review[6], as reported in chapter 2 of this book, served to clarify these issues. While implementation of the report's recommendations would improve the legal framework for IPR from the point of view of educational usage, the importance of appropriate licence agreements will not be diminished.

JISC Collections is a company established by the JISC to negotiate with commercial providers of digital content on behalf of UK higher and further education institutions. As a basis of all the agreements it negotiates JISC Collections uses the 'JISC Model Licence', which seeks to protect the interests of commercial owners of content, while ensuring that online resources can be used effectively in research and education.

When it negotiates licence agreements with owners of digital images, JISC Collections will seek to secure terms and conditions of use that will help to ensure that staff and students in higher and further education institutions can use digital images and embed them in their activities with confidence. The specific terms and conditions of use that JISC Collections sees as essential in the context of 'educational' use are as follows.

All images must be copyright cleared for educational use. Once an institution has agreed to the terms of a licence, all staff and all students of the institution must be able to use the images (in conjunction with educational activities such as teaching or research) freely and without further authorisation. Such permissions are essential for the creative use of images in education.

Post-cancellation access to downloaded images must be allowed. After termination of a licence agreement, institutions must be able to retain the digital images that have been embedded in virtual and electronic learning materials. One of the greatest barriers to using subscription collections is a licence agreement that requires users to destroy all downloaded images when the licence terminates. Teachers and lecturers will not embed images in their teaching if there is the risk that they will have to destroy them should their institution be unable to afford the ongoing subscription fees required for the licence agreement.

Offline image viewing must be allowed. Users must be able to view and display images offline and they must be able to download images into standard applications such as Microsoft Office Power Point and into open source software solutions. Offline viewing is essential – very few lecturers or teachers want to risk the availability of an online connection in the lecture theatre or classroom.

Some providers of digital image collections do allow for offline viewing but only within proprietary software. Such software can be difficult to manipulate and is not necessarily compatible with other software used in the preparation and creation of teaching materials. Furthermore, permissions and authorisation for 'plug-ins' or downloads of proprietary software can be frustratingly difficult to obtain in many higher and further education institutions.

Users – in conjunction with teaching and learning activities – must be allowed to make creative use of images, including electronic enhancement, modification, manipulation or combination with other free-use images. For demonstration and instruction it is essential that lecturers and teachers are able to make such modifications in order to 'make the point'.

As part of their educational activities, students must be able to make derivative works from the licensed images and to include those works in their project work and dissertations. The manipulation of images is a creative activity and is required in many courses in the visual and performing arts. The Radio 1 Superstar VJs[7] is part of a new kind of service the BBC is piloting, and a good example of the creative use of image collections now being allowed under the Creative Archive Licence.

Deposit in Jorum of images incorporated in teaching materials must be allowed. Jorum is a free online repository service for teaching and support staff in UK further and higher education institutions, helping to build a community for the sharing, re-use and re-purposing of learning and teaching materials. Teaching materials are expensive and time-consuming to create and teaching staff frequently need to include images in these materials. Jorum allows such materials to be shared. The provenance of images embedded in such materials will be cited, and access to Jorum is limited to members of higher and further education institutions in the UK.

The MIDESS project

MIDESS[8] (Management of Images in a Distributed Environment with Shared Services) is a JISC-funded project to explore the management of digitised content in an institutional and cross-institutional context across the entire life cycle through the development of a distributed digital repository infrastructure pilot. This pilot infrastructure, as well as providing an environment for examining a range of issues for implementing digital content management services, could serve as a model for co-ordination of future distributed national digitisation activities. A range of image sources and subject domains will be incorporated, and issues to be explored include:

- metadata standards;

- sharing and re-use;

- interoperability with enterprise content management architectures;

- evaluation of requirements for centralised metadata harvesting service.

The two-year project – led by University of Leeds with partners University of Birmingham, London School of Economics and University College London – is due to complete in summer 2007. Many of the projects focusing on one or more of the individual life-cycle stages will be working with MIDESS as well as with TASI to achieve a co-ordinated approach to the development of systems, processes, tools and guidance.

In the Create/Acquire stage of the life cycle

Recognising the importance of strategic resource creation, we need to move beyond a focus on the individual goals of organisations and practitioners to taking account of reusability – and this includes taking account *at the time of creation* of requirements for preservation for long-term (and even medium-term) continuing access. We should recognise that some collections do need to be commissioned. TASI will continue to play an important role in supporting digital-image creation, whether through digitisation or the creation of born-digital images. In addition, possible areas for further study may be identified. One outstanding question is why people choose one image-authoring or creation tool rather than another. A comparison of the functionality, utility and usability of tools for the creation of raster and vector images might be useful.

Digitisation and collection enrichment

It is important to note here that the JISC is currently moving towards a more strategic and also user-driven approach to access to digital content. For example, the second phase of JISC Digitisation Programme[9] will generate a rich seam of resources for education and research, and these resources will be created with more emphasis than before on the learning and research context. The JISC will not only encourage all digitisation projects to work more proactively than previously to capture user requirements, but will also support them in doing so. The approach was initiated even before the selection of projects through a series of digitisation-user-needs workshops held in Bristol, Glasgow, Leeds and London in February and March of 2006. These workshops brought out a number of common themes, as recorded by Rightscom[10] in their April 2006 report, that echo concerns arising across the digital-image studies reported in this book:

- functionality in access to and use of digital resources;

- discovery, in relation both to how findable digital resources are and the degree to which existing collections are connected to each other and to new collections to be created;

- sustainability in terms of maintenance, continuing availability and further development of collections created;

- the level of consultation with potential users on the value of new initiatives across subjects and sectors, but also in terms of value for money.

Recommendations based on these conclusions were used to improve the process of selecting and planning projects for the second phase of digitisation. An important improvement was the increased level of consultation with potential users as part of the selection process, going beyond the usual community-based proposal-review panel. Although many of the funded projects will create digital images, some are of particular interest for digital image creation. The Scott Polar Research Institute[11] at Cambridge University, for example, will make a repository of historic images and text available for learning, teaching and research through the project Discovering the Poles – Historic Polar Images 1845-1960. The source for the images is an archive of more than 20,000 extremely fragile photographic negatives, while the texts are manuscript reports and personal papers of members of the Scott and Shackleton expedition teams. These resources will be set in

"Come on, Sir—admit you hate me."

"Come on, Sir–admit you hate me."
© British Cartoon Archive.

context through a series of interpretive web pages and e-learning and online learning resources. The British Cartoon Archive Digitisation (BCAD)[12] project at the University of Kent's Centre for the Study of Cartoons and Caricature will digitise the Carl Giles Archive, making it possible to browse the largest online archive of cartoons in the UK by linking these 15,000 original cartoons and cartoon prints, 75,000 individual published prints and about 5,000 digital images of paperwork from the Carl Giles Archive together, and also to the more than 123,000 digitised and catalogued cartoons by other British cartoonists already in the centre's database.

A draft JISC Digitisation Strategy sets out some of the principles whereby the JISC may select content to digitise on behalf of its community, ensure that this content is appropriate and wherever possible address stated gaps in current provision. The difficulty as always is gathering evidence to support cases for what new resources should be digitised. However, in going forward, the gaps and issues highlighted in this book will be a good starting point in the images area, and will help to drive priorities. For example, as part of the draft JISC Digitisation Strategy, a number of principles have been proposed, as follows. In consultation with our users, the JISC will give priority to the digitisation of collections that:

- make the hidden visible: enable access to and use of difficult or impossible-to-access collections;
- address a recognised need or gap within learning, teaching or research provision;
- map to a particular area of the curriculum or research interest;
- inspire new avenues of research or new approaches within learning and teaching;
- contribute to creating critical mass within a given area or help to create a theme across previously unassociated materials;
- would not otherwise be funded or be able to attract significant funding from other sources;
- are at risk from being lost to the higher and further education community through sale, deterioration or disaggregation.

The JISC will aspire to create digital collections that are:

- standards based: employ and develop standards for digital capture and description;
- interoperable: deploy the standards specified within the JISC Information Environment for interoperability and offer excellence in resource discovery;
- user focused: have been created with a high level of user engagement, offer a high-quality user experience, and where users have been actively engaged in the design of interfaces and delivery mechanisms;
- innovative: explore new approaches and embrace current developments in technology;
- contextualised: are accompanied by contextual examples to help take-up for learning and research;
- sustainable: where suitable service provision and business models can be put in place to ensure future sustainability.

The Strategic Content Alliance

Work is also underway within the JISC Executive to draw together a number of strands of activity that should ultimately mean that users within the JISC community are offered a more coherent and richer set of digital resources. Of particular note is the Strategic Content Alliance[13]. The rationale for its work, as stated on the JISC website, is as follows:

"The rapid growth and development of electronic content offers enormous and ever-growing possibilities for all citizens in the UK. But for this country to realise the full potential of the web, and for each citizen to realise their own potential – in the workplace, in their places of learning and in the home – the full range of online content needs to be made available to all, quickly, easily and in a form appropriate to individuals' needs.

Organisations in different sectors are making significant amounts of online content available to their respective communities – in health, education, museums, archives, research, public libraries and so on. However, the barriers between sectors mean that not all this content is accessible to all who might need it or want it. Too much remains hidden amongst the low-quality information that clutters the web and behind technical, commercial and administrative barriers.

A number of key public sector bodies also recognise that parallel investment has taken place in the digital educational assets, infrastructure and services to support enhanced engagement with online resources for formal and informal learning. There is clearly a risk that without much greater common working our respective contributions in providing access to new digital resources will be limited to individual branded networks, and that users will not fully benefit from the central investment that has been made in these initiatives. Overcoming these barriers requires concerted action on the part of all organisations in the field."

Strategic Content Alliance. in JISC. What we do at http://www.jisc.ac.uk/whatwedo/themes/eresources/contentalliance.aspx

In driving forward this activity, the JISC is working with its partners in media, health, research, the cultural sector and life-long learning. This work particularly recognises that inter-agency and (at a higher level) inter-UK government collaboration is a key to cracking the issue of access to digital content for the JISC community and others in the public sector. Certain challenges are high on the horizon for this initiative, one of which is the lack of coherence driving the selection of content for digitisation across the public sector. Other challenges that have been particularly noted are the lack of common support across the public sector for expertise in digitisation and lack of common standards and resource discovery solutions.

The JISC is also beginning work to draw together activities in the following three areas:

- content licensing (through the JISC Collections company);

- access to community resources via the JISC Repositories and Digital Preservation Programme, especially those within UK HE and FE institutions;

- content created through the JISC Digitisation programmes.

It is clear that the more joined up we can be across areas of activity in the e-content arena, the more quickly and efficiently we will be able to deliver our vision of access to high-quality content (including digital images) across the HE and FE learning and research community.

All of these activities should support the vision for access to digital images that is at the heart of this publication. Of course, if we are realistic, it is important to recognise that in some areas the rate of change will not be particularly fast. Incremental development will be supported by a number of activities sponsored by the JISC, but the main change will come from within the JISC community itself in having the skills base and the organisational and individual capacity to fully embrace the potential of digital image resources.

Tracks to "Antares"
NASA.

In the Deposit/Ingest stage of the life cycle

Tools and guidance

Although technology is not the main issue – most barriers to sharing are social, legal and organisational – tools are needed that make it possible to get value for the community from the sharing of image collections while also taking account of 'branding' issues. The provenance of the images being shared must be made clear; so must the context within which they are being made available for use. This requires systems that allow sharing, but preserve personal and/or organisational identity. In support of this goal, we need tools and guidance that facilitate deposit and ingest processes, and that demonstrate the benefits of the metadata and make metadata easy to create.

Innovative ingest tools. Especially relevant in this stage of the life cycle is the Innovation and Tools strand of the JISC Repositories and Preservation Programme, which funds projects developing tools that can enhance the use of repositories or digital information systems, tools that may be either software or model practices. The CAIRO[14] and SOURCE[15] projects are funded in this strand. CAIRO (Complex Archive Ingest for Repository Objects) will develop an open-source tool for ingesting complex collections of born-digital material into a preservation repository. The resulting tool will be available for use in similar situations. As images are often part of the type of complex archival collections for which this tool is being developed and which will be used to test it, this could be of benefit within the architecture developed for distributed image collections. The 18-month project, led by the University of Oxford and with partners University of Manchester and the Wellcome Library, is due to complete in spring 2008.

The SOURCE (Sharing Objects Under Repository Control with Everyone) project will create a pair of tools that could have value for the infrastructure supporting the vision for digital image in terms of the Deposit/Ingest stage. The tools to be developed are a bulk migration tool to get objects from one repository into another and the 'plug' for interoperability between repositories in terms of the import and export of object formats. SOURCE is due to complete in October 2008. Led by Birkbeck College, project partners are the Bloomsbury Colleges Consortium (Institute of Education, London School of Hygiene and Tropical Medicine, School of Oriental and African Studies, School of Pharmacy, Royal Veterinary College and Birkbeck College), Jorum (National Learning Object Repository – UK) and the OKI project (The Open Knowledge Initiative).

Selection and retention criteria. Best-practice guidelines that support long-term management of, and access to, images are required. In order to produce such guidance, a number of basic questions must be answered. We cannot simply assume that because a digital image has been created it is worth keeping, so guidance on selection and retention criteria that take account of cost models and the value produced is needed. The case studies of image use described below, in the section on the Use and Re-Use stage of the life cycle, will also have relevance to this aspect of the Deposit/Ingest stage.

Metadata standards

Repository metadata schemas are not seen as well suited to digital image collections. There are no accepted standards across the broad field of digital images for the mark-up of images, especially vector images. There is a consensus that a Dublin Core application profile for the deposit of images within repositories is required to allow for consistent search and retrieval. JISC will actively seek ways to support the development of such a profile, in consultation with the Dublin Core standards community, organisations and services including TASI, AHDS and UKOLN, and through the MIDESS project and the new Defining Image Access[16] project described below in the section on the Discovery stage of the life cycle. Also relevant here is the AHDS-led project, Investigating the Significant Properties of Electronic Content over Time (INSPECT)[17]. INSPECT is discussed below in the Preserve stage section.

In the Discover stage of the life cycle

The Discover stage covers not only finding an image, but also getting the image so that it can be used. The Discovery to Delivery strand within the Repositories and Preservation Programme is funding projects that develop solutions or demonstrate issues that will help offer improved discovery to delivery. Some funded projects, while having a broader scope than image resources, will still have potential to improve digital-image discovery. Others relate more specifically to images, including the Defining Image Access project, the Visual Materials and Sound Portal: Scoping Study and Demonstrator Project[18] and the Rich Tags[19] project.

Metadata for resource discovery – tools and guidance

While metadata is required across the full digital-images life cycle, metadata for resource discovery is particularly important for facilitating the use of digital images. We need to explore the relative advantages of content-based and metadata-based image retrieval and a combination of the two approaches. (See also the discussion of content-based image retrieval in chapter 2.)

Rich Tags: Supporting better exploration of digital repositories with semantic social tagging. The Rich Tags project will investigate how cross-repository browsing/exploration can be assisted via social, *semantic* tagging mechanisms, and will deliver a test framework and web services both to investigate the use of and to deploy services for such *meaningful* mechanisms. Note the emphasis here on the semantic, as much as the social aspects of tagging. Many community-based sharing sites allow users to add tags to their artefacts, and in some cases to the artefacts provided by others, to give them a more personal meaning that can be shared and used publicly among the community. The possibilities for enriched discovery metadata created in this way are particularly relevant to digital images, as a picture may perhaps have many different meanings in addition to its meaning for its originator. The Rich Tags project is led by the Intelligence, Agent and Multimedia Group, Electronics and Computer Science, University of Southampton.

Pathways to discovery

Discovery issues other than those related to metadata are also significant for the Discover stage of the life cycle. Perhaps the most significant is the fragmentation of access. As discussed in chapter 2 and brought out in the studies reported here, there is no one place to go to find out about what digital images are available for education and research. With many sources available, and many perhaps outside the awareness of potential users, there is a great temptation to fall back on one familiar pathway such as Google image searching and hope for the best. A number of relevant projects are currently underway or recently have been granted funding that will support unified access to digital images for use in education and research. These include, in particular, the MIDESS project described above, the Defining Image Access project, and the Visual Materials and Sound Portal: Scoping Study and Demonstrator Project.

Defining Image Access project. Defining Image Access is a six-month project to analyse the requirements for interoperable discovery and delivery of image data stored in DSpace, EPrints and Fedora-based institutional repositories. Led by Dr David Shotton, Reader in Image Bioinformatics at University of Oxford, this project will create data webs for images held in these repositories. (In a data web, metadata harvesting is used to discover data and information from independent sources.) The project will:

- examine the differences between software structures and semantics of the repository systems and how they affect image storage;

- explore metadata standards and schemas for handling image data and the existing metadata descriptors for images within repository holdings and their semantic consistency across repositories to determine how and where these metadata standards might need to be extended or improved and then to define the requirements for an image data web core ontology that will provide a basis for linking data across different repositories' sources;

- undertake a survey of lightweight software tools that will permit the creation of a central data-web metadata registry and design the operational logic for data-web functionality.

Project partners are the universities of Oxford, Cambridge and Southampton; Imperial College of Science, Technology and Medicine, London; and UKOLN, University of Bath. The project will collaborate with Intute[20] on its JISC-funded Institutional Repositories search service[21] development. (Intute, formerly known as the RDN, is a free online service for access to selected, evaluated resources for education and research. It is funded by the JISC, with additional funding from some of the UK research councils.) The Defining Image Access project will also collaborate with the MIDESS project and the JISC TASI service. In 2007 it will deliver a report with recommendations for best practice and implementation guidelines for the creation of data webs and an account of how they can enhance image interoperability between institutional repositories.

Portal for discovery and sharing. The Visual and Sound Materials (VSM) portal scoping study and demonstrator project has the potential to enhance access to available collections and encourage sharing of collections. Undertaken by EDINA, the first phase of the project began in the autumn of 2005 and phase two is due to complete toward the end of 2007. A response to the challenges of fragmentation of access, the VSM project's demonstrator system will pave the way for a possible pilot service. In the first phase of VSM, the focus was a scoping study exploring the functional, software, collection and user-needs requirements of a portal to cross-search and access still images and time-based media from within a single user interface. The second phase is focusing on demonstrator development, while continuing to keep a watch on metadata, technology and standards progress, investigating legal issues and reviewing portal software.

The VSM project objectives are well aligned with the vision for image provision in UK tertiary education and the recommendations arising from the CLIC and *the* Digital Picture studies. An important question addressed by this project is whether there are significant advantages in providing access to still images and time-based visual and audio resources through a single portal. There are arguments both for and against this approach, and the VSM demonstrator will provide an environment for testing the validity of these arguments. There is also the question of the extent to which such a portal should facilitate activities other than discovery through delivery. For example, it could provide an application interface (API) to make it possible for third parties to development applications for content access and use that would interact with the VSM demonstrator.

In the Use and Re-Use stage of the life cycle

Learning more about image creators, users and usage

The studies found that most use of images is simple, and that this is the case across many domains, although there are differences between teaching and research in terms of simplicity and sophistication of use as well as the types of uses. Beyond the illustrative use of images in teaching lie many opportunities, including collaborative art with digital images, which is already beginning to be exploited, and research, including using images to aid 'forensic' examination of original material through digital imaging, and experience in the astrophysics, geospatial and other fields where digital images are part of the basic research data.

A small study in a defined geographic area suggests that images are more likely to be re-used than other types of digital resources, being by a significant margin the most commonly created and shared. The findings of the WM-Share[22] project looking at supply and demand of various types of shared content in the West Midlands are interesting when taken in conjunction with the studies reported here. Further knowledge of the creators, users and usage of images is needed to inform decisions across a range of issues, including resource allocation, commissioning of collections, collection development, licensing of commercial collections, collection management and preservation. These are considerations that should also be applied in the Create/Acquire stage of the digital-image life cycle.

Case studies of image use

Case studies of current pedagogical and research uses of images, whether digitised or born-digital, can be developed as one way of capturing such knowledge. It is also important to recognise that different subject groups may have differing needs, and to provide balanced support across a range of disciplines. Significant properties – what is important in terms of the different subject areas – will inform decisions about creation, selection and retention of, and metadata for, digital images. There is a need to look at the value that the use, management and preservation of digital images has added, or can potentially add, in any particular subject area. While a further area for exploration is the cross-domain potential of digital image use, it should be recognised that academics who don't want to 'join in' national repositories may be more willing to engage at subject level early in the implementation process. Work undertaken should also attempt to present a balanced perspective on image use in teaching and in research.

Funding has been agreed to undertake case studies in five key subject areas to be selected in consultation with the Higher Education Academy (HEA) and TASI. The case studies will focus on how images are used, and how community image collections can support this use by offering facilities to deposit and share images owned by the higher education community. The subject areas identified as candidates for these case studies are Art History, Medicine, Geology, Bioscience, Structural Engineering, Fashion Design, Philosophical and Religious Studies, Psychology, and History, Classics and Archaeology. Each of these areas represents a domain in which images are key resources, and where sharing images within the higher education community would offer significant benefits. Some of them are represented by HEA subject centres, which have been involved in recent HEA and JISC Digital e-Learning (DeL) programme-funded projects that have looked at image sharing, and so would allow the further benefit of building on these experiences.

An 'action research' approach will be taken, in which changes in practice (informed by the results of the CLIC study) are made in collaboration with those working in the subject areas identified, and the process and outcomes documented. It will be important to recruit help and advice from those with specialist knowledge. This will be achieved by working closely with TASI and relevant HEA subject centres in planning and executing this work. A brief report of each case study will be produced, showing how the CLIC recommendations can be taken forward in a variety of subject areas. In addition, activities will be supported to present the case-study work to stakeholders. The work will be completed during 2007.

In the Preserve stage of the life cycle

The high level of variety and complexity in digital images is a key issue in their preservation. For example, and in particular, see the discussion of the different issues involved in the preservation of vector and raster images in chapter 6. We need to know who is creating digital-image standards, and why, in order to make sensible decisions about preservation. Best-practice guidelines that support long-term management of, and access to, images are required. A demonstration of the gap in support for good practice is that there seems to be no evidence to confirm the commonly made assumption that the TIFF format is preferable for preservation. We need to test such assumptions. The image-archiving study and a companion moving-image archiving study found that while much research supports the preservation of video resources, little research about the preservation of digital images has been done.

Significant properties for preservation of digital objects

The JISC has now funded Investigating the Significant Properties of Electronic Content Over Time (INSPECT) within the Repositories and Preservation Strand B: Tools and Innovation element of the Capital Programme. INSPECT will look at the significant properties of digital objects, including raster images. Significant properties are those aspects of the digital object that must be preserved over time in order for it to remain accessible and meaningful. The various properties of a digital object may be categorised as content, context, appearance (e.g. layout, colour), behaviour (e.g. interaction, functionality) and structure (e.g. pagination, sections).

Deciding which aspects of each of these categories must be preserved over time is essential to proper preservation planning, and INSPECT will examine the whole concept of significant properties and clearly articulate a complete and appropriate working definition. (The concept was raised and explored in

Ice, ship and men
© Scott Polar Research Institute.

the earlier Cedars[23] and CAMiLEON[24] projects.) Once the concept is properly understood and articulated, the project will also examine a range of digital object types to analyse, assess and specify the significant properties of each, including raster images, digital audio, structured text and email. The Arts and Humanities Data Service (AHDS) and The National Archive (TNA) are partners in this project, with AHDS as the lead partner, and the project is scheduled to be completed in mid-October 2008.

Investigation of the significant properties of digital objects is critical to establishing best practice approaches to preserving digital objects. A proper appreciation of which characteristics of digital objects must be preserved will not only assist and influence the development of improved preservation tools; it will also inform future work on developing common standards across the preservation community. In addition, significant properties are a useful starting point to develop our understanding of complex digital objects such as vector images, for which little digital preservation research or practical work has been undertaken. E-learning objects, software and moving images are further examples of such complex objects.

To complement the INSPECT project and expand the portfolio of the digital objects being examined, the JISC plans a further series of studies investigating and analysing the significant properties of individual complex objects. Although the scope of some of the object types is yet to be defined, vector images and moving images are the foci of two studies. The studies will take place from June through November 2007. As the work package within the INSPECT project which develops and expounds the concept of significant properties will conclude post March 2007, the new studies will be able to benefit from and build on this work.

Other initiatives

In addition, the JISC is encouraging the projects it funds to contribute data to the PRONOM file-format registry developed by The National Archives, thus adding various file formats to the basic range it already covers. This would include image file formats. And although the primary focus of the Digital Curation Centre (DCC)[25] is on scientific data, it is recognised that images are prime scientific data objects. Therefore, over time the DCC is likely to add some image standards to the DIFFUSE database and to add entries that relate to digital-image preservation to its external resource and tools database. The DCC has commissioned a curation manual instalment on the curation of born-digital art, which will cover the preservation of digital images to some extent. A more general DCC briefing paper on the curation of born-digital art is in the pipeline.

The vision revisited

The IWG envisioned the UK education community provided with long-term access to the digital-image resources that it needs, in convenient, flexible and easy-to-use ways. It further envisioned an ideal future when provision would:

- be free at the point of use;
- comply with common open standards;
- cover the broadest range of possible subject areas;
- have copyright clarity;
- be sustainable;
- support maximum usage at all levels of teaching, learning and research.

Although some building blocks for such provision are in place, and the initiatives described above will improve the foundations, much more work will be needed to realise the vision. The evidence of the past ten years is that the will to do this work and the talent and dedication required are abundant in the higher and further education community (especially as represented by the IWG, TASI and AHDS) and in its partners in other sectors such as museums, archives and national libraries.

References

1. Jorum
    http://www.jorum.ac.uk/

2. TASI (Technical Advisory Service for Images)
    http://www.tasi.ac.uk/

3. HEA (Higher Education Academy) Subject Centre Distributed e-Learning (DeL)
    Programme Projects
    (This includes projects developing image banks for specific subjects.)
    http://www.heacademy.ac.uk/1877.htm

4. bigfoto.com – Pictures free Download
    http://www.bigfoto.com/

5. AICT – Art Images for College Teaching: A free-Use Educational Resource
    http://www.arthist.umn.edu/aict/html/

6. Gowers Review of Intellectual Property. HM Treasury – Independent reviews
    http://www.hm-treasury.gov.uk/independent_reviews/gowers_review_
    intellectual_property/gowersreview_index.cfm

7. Radio 1 Superstar VJs
    http://www.bbc.co.uk/calc/radio1/

8. MIDESS (Management of Images in a Distributed Environment with Shared
    Services)
    http://www.leeds.ac.uk/library/midess/index.html

9. JISC Digitisation Programme
    http://www.jisc.ac.uk/digitisation

10. *Report on JISC digitisation user need focus group discussions held in February and
    March 2006*. Rightscom Ltd, London, 19 April 2006.
    The report is available via a link from the JISC Digitisation Programme events
    web page: Workshops on User(s) Need(s) for future digitisation of collections –
    Report by Rightscom
    http://www.jisc.ac.uk/whatwedo/programmes/programme_digitisation/
    programme_events.aspx

11. Scott Polar Research Institute: Discovering the Poles – Historic polar images
    http://www.jisc.ac.uk/whatwedo/programmes/programme_digitisation/
    polar.aspx

12. British Cartoon Archive digitisation project
    http://www.jisc.ac.uk/whatwedo/programmes/programme_digitisation/
    cartoons.aspx

13. Strategic Content Alliance
    http://www.jisc.ac.uk/whatwedo/themes/eresources/contentalliance.aspx

14. CAIRO (Complex Archive Ingest for Repository Objects)
    http://cairo.paradigm.ac.uk/about/index.html

    http://www.jisc.ac.uk/whatwedo/programmes/programme_rep_pres/cairo.
    aspx

15. SOURCE: Sharing Objects Under Repository Control with Everyone
    http://www.source.bbk.ac.uk/

16. Defining Image Access
http://www.jisc.ac.uk/whatwedo/programmes/programme_rep_pres/
defining_image_access.aspx

17. INSPECT (Investigating the Significant Properties of Electronic Content Over Time)
http://www.jisc.ac.uk/whatwedo/programmes/programme_rep_pres/
inspect.aspx

18. The Visual and Sound Materials (VSM) portal scoping study and demonstrator project
http://www.jisc.ac.uk/whatwedo/programmes/programme_portals/project_
vsmportal.aspx

19. Rich Tags: Supporting better exploration of digital repositories with semantic social tagging
http://mspace.fm/projects/richtags/

http://www.jisc.ac.uk/whatwedo/programmes/programme_rep_pres/rich_
tags.aspx

20. Intute
http://www.intute.ac.uk/

21. Institutional Repositories search service (in Intute: Current projects involving Intute and its Subject Groups)
http://www.intute.ac.uk/projects.html

22. WM-Share (West Midlands Share Project) Promoting the Use of Shared Content in the West Midlands
http://www2.worc.ac.uk/wm-share/

23. Cedars project (CURL Exemplars in Digital Archives, April 1998 – March 2002)
http://www.leeds.ac.uk/cedars/

24. CAMiLEON project (Creative Archiving at Michigan and Leeds Emulating the Old On the New, October 1999 – September 2003)
http://www.si.umich.edu/CAMILEON/

25. DCC (Digital Curation Centre)
http://www.dcc.ac.uk/
DCC Digital Curation Manual
http://www.dcc.ac.uk/resource/curation-manual/

Further reading

Hedström, M., Lee, C. 'Significant Properties of Digital Objects: Definitions, Applications, Implications' in *Proceedings of the DLM-Forum 2002*, pp218-223, European Communities, Barcelona. Available online:
http://www.ils.unc.edu/callee/sigprops_dlm2002.pdf

Manual annotation of image data. *DCC Forum*. March 2006
http://forum.dcc.ac.uk/viewtopic.php?t=155

Notay, B., and Grout, C., 'Looking For More than Text'. *Ariadne*, Issue 45
http://www.ariadne.ac.uk/issue45/notay/

Appendix

The images used in this book

I wanted to briefly explain the thinking behind the selection of the images in the book. Some of the images have been chosen to represent the image collections that have been licensed through JISC Collections or funded by JISC and are now available to the education community and some are there to emphasise the text.

The first image of the book is of a group of Jewish refugees arriving in Antwerp on their way to America. Unlike many images of refugees, they are smiling. They are on a journey into the unknown but when I see this image, I feel as though they are embracing change. I found this image hopeful and liked that idea that it could represent the journey that the education community has to take to embrace the use of digital images in their everyday study and work.

The image of the full earth and earth with the robot arm are two of my favourites. The Images Working Group Vision aims to be all encompassing, and although it is clichéd to say it, you can't understand the whole without understanding all the bits that make that make up that whole. The perspective offered by the robot arm helps you to realise the sheer scale of the earth or if you will, the digital image environment.

In Chapter 1, if you are confused as to why a picture of thousands of turkeys was chosen, well here's the reason why. Throughout the vision we use the term reservoir and we wanted something to represent that term that wasn't water, that wasn't a repository but a collection and we thought that a nice way to show that would be a collection of turkeys on display! Another of my favourites is 'One of the Four Foundations of Modern Living'. Imagine life previous to electricity, when it arrived it was the dawn of the modern age. Now electricity is something that we can't live without and I expect that soon we will feel the same about digital cameras, digital images and digital image collections.

In Chapter 2 we use a variety of images to demonstrate the landscape, which differs greatly from the image of the farmers and their dogs in 1937. The landscape we face now is a digital environment where those most at comfort are the children that are growing up surrounded by online resources and technology.

In Chapter 3 there is another interesting NASA image of the crop circles in Kansas, it could almost be a piece of art. To me, this image perfectly represents the mind-boggling landscape of IPR, content providers and licensing that users have to navigate through to find the digital images that meet their needs.

When trying to think about what images would best demonstrate a community-led initiative as described in Chapter 4, I realised that what I wanted to portray was a community of sharing. All the images in this chapter have been submitted by members (and past members) of the JISC Images Working Group and I am grateful to them for sharing their colourful records of their travels around the world. Fostering this attitude of willingness to share within the community helps us move one step closer to achieving the Vision.

There are no images in Chapter 5 except the one that shows 'image withdrawn'. This is to make the point that restrictions on clinical images are often so many that it is impossible to use such images in the teaching, learning and research environment. Overcoming these barriers is essential but complex and will require further investigation.

Preserving and archiving images is essential and Chapter 6 includes a variety of images from the Institution of Civil Engineers and from the Pidgeon Digital collection. These images signify that preservation depends on the type of image and the need for that image to preserved, whether it is born-digital, digitised, vector or raster.

Images incorporated in the last chapter all represent next steps. There is a lovely image from the Archaeology Data Service where archaeologists are encouraged to donate their images for sharing and all images can be used for teaching, learning and research. In addition, digitised images from a variety of collections that have received JISC funding through the digitisation programme are included. These collections have all been voted by the community as having great value and it is fantastic that JISC is providing funding to ensure that these images are shared and used for education. What's next? Well the last images in the book show that Scott made it to the South Pole and man explored the moon, now its time for us all to collaborate and take the next steps forward to help realise the Vision for digital images in education.

Caren Milloy

Index

Page numbers in **bold** indicate discussions of a topic, in *italic* indicate illustrations.